United States
Department of
Agriculture

Forest Service

Southern
Research Station

Resource Bulletin
SRS–145

Southern Pulpwood Production, 2007

Tony G. Johnson,
Carolyn D. Steppleton,
and James W. Bentley

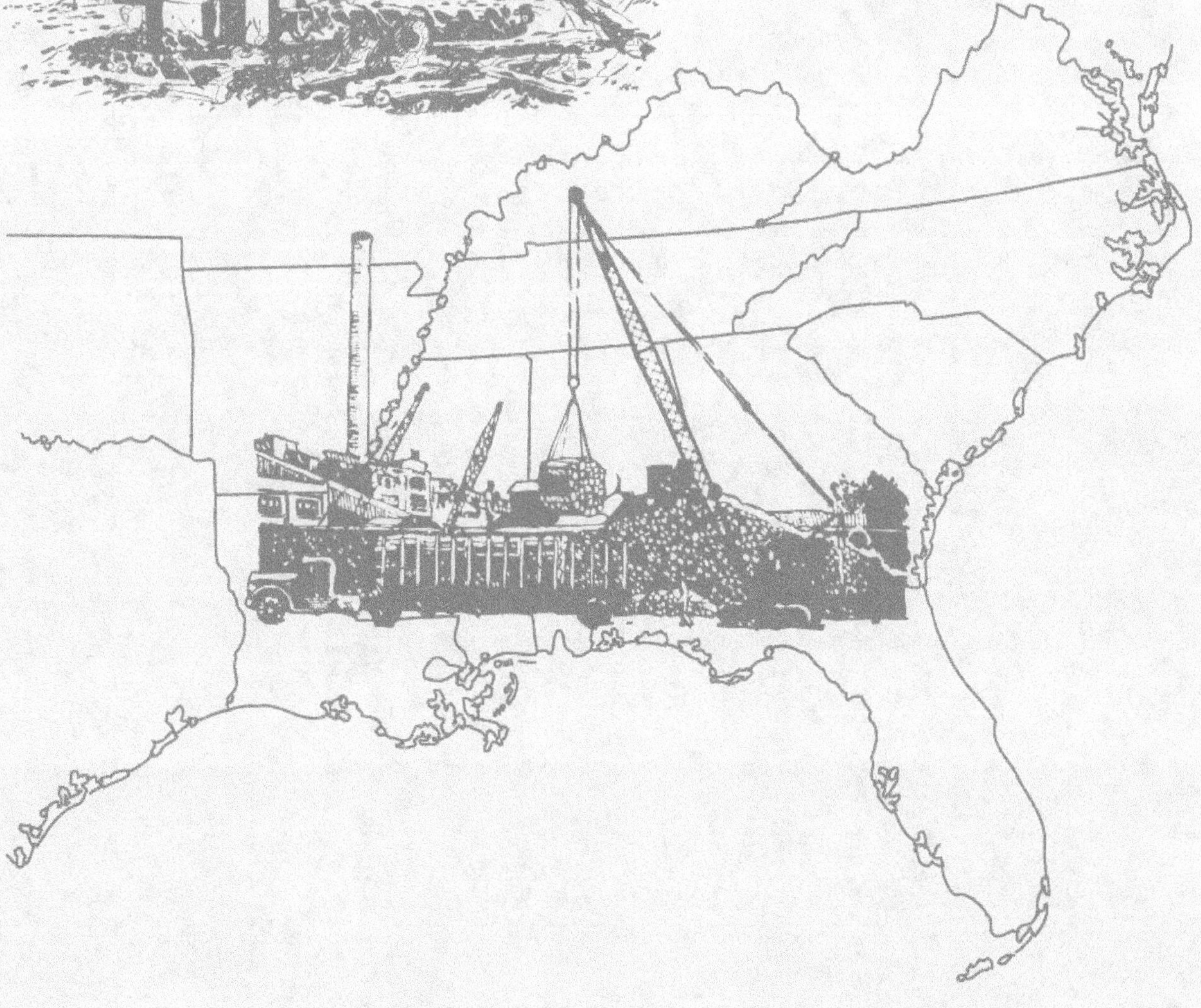

In this report:

Note: All tables in this report are available in Microsoft® Excel workbook files. Upon request these files will be supplied in the format the customer requests.

The use of trade or firm names in this publication is for reader information and does not imply endorsement by the U.S. Department of Agriculture of any product or service.

April 2009

Southern Research Station
200 W.T. Weaver Blvd.
Asheville, NC 28804

Southern Pulpwood Production, 2007

Tony G. Johnson, Forester
Forest Inventory and Analysis,
Forest Service, Southern Research Station
U.S. Department of Agriculture, Knoxville, TN

and

Carolyn D. Steppleton, Statistical Assistant
Forest Inventory and Analysis
Forest Service, Southern Research Station
U.S. Department of Agriculture, Asheville, NC

and

James W. Bentley, Forester
Forest Inventory and Analysis,
Forest Service, Southern Research Station
U.S. Department of Agriculture, Knoxville, TN

Introduction

This annual publication presents the findings of a 100-percent canvass of pulpmills that draw roundwood or wood residues from the 13 Southern States. Canvass data are compiled, analyzed, and reported annually by the Forest Service, U.S. Department of Agriculture, Southern Research Station. In 2007, 82 of the 87 mills canvassed responded. Past canvass data and other sources of information were used for mills that did not respond. Mill data reported in nonstandard units were converted to standard cords using regional conversion factors. All production figures are reported in cords and do not include pulpwood that is exported out of the country. Production expressed in equivalent green tons is reported in tables A.1, A.3, and A.7 through A.19.

Pulpwood

Total southern pulpwood production, which includes both roundwood chipped at pulp mills or at independent chip mills, and other primary industry mill residues, was up 2 percent in 2007 to 65.7 million cords, or 173.8 million green tons (table A.1). At 47.3 million cords, softwood production increased 1.3 million cords, or 3 percent. Hardwood production was down nearly 2 percent, from 18.7 million cords to 18.4 million cords. Softwood roundwood and residues combined accounted for 72 percent of the total Southern pulpwood production, while hardwoods accounted for the remaining 28 percent (table A.2). By comparison, total Southern pulpwood production was 13

percent lower than the record volume of 75.9 million cords (200.9 million green tons) reported in 1997.

In 2007, the South Central region's (Alabama, Arkansas, Kentucky, Louisiana, Mississippi, Oklahoma, Tennessee, and Texas) pulpwood production increased >1 percent from 34.9 million cords to 35.4 million cords. Softwood pulpwood production increased nearly 3 percent in the region; however, this increase was partially offset by a 1-percent decline in hardwood production of nearly 157,000 cords. The South Central region's production was down 17 percent, or nearly 7.2 million cords (18.9 million green tons) from the peak year of 1997. Between 1997 and 2007 the South Central region has lost 10 pulpmills and 11 percent of its pulping capacity.

The Southeast's (Florida, Georgia, North Carolina, South Carolina, and Virginia) pulpwood production was up nearly 2 percent from 29.8 million cords to 30.4 million cords. Softwood pulpwood production was up 3 percent in this region, or 674,000 cords, while hardwood production was down >127,000 cords, or 2 percent. The Southeast region's pulpwood production declined 9 percent, or 3.0 million cords (8.1 million green tons) from the peak year of 1997. Between 1997 and 2007 this region has lost six pulpmills and 9 percent of its pulping capacity.

Alabama's pulpwood production increased 1 percent in 2007 to 10.6 million cords, and led the South in total pulpwood production (fig. 1). Georgia's production increased 3 percent from 10.2 million cords to 10.5 million cords. Production in Mississippi was up 4 percent to 7.4 million cords, while

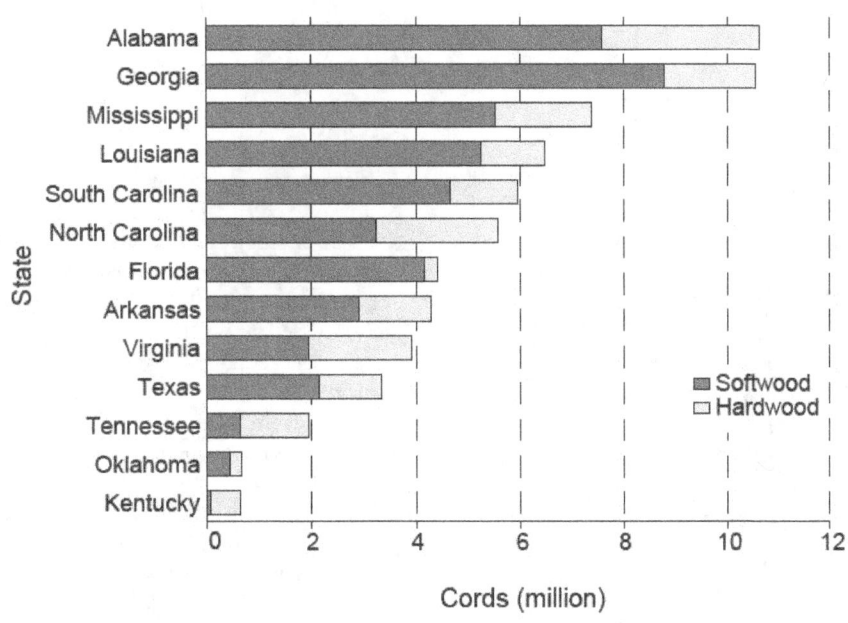

Figure 1—Pulpwood production by State and broad species, 2007.

Louisiana's production was up 2 percent to 6.5 million cords. Pulpwood production in South Carolina dropped 2 percent to 5.9 million cords. Collectively, these five States accounted for nearly 41.0 million cords, or 62 percent of the South's total production in 2007 (table A.3).

Roundwood

Roundwood pulpwood continues to be the primary fiber source used in pulp manufacture in the South, accounting for 72 percent of the total southern pulpwood production in 2007, the same as in 2006 and 2005, but compared to 74 percent in 2004 and 72 percent of total pulpwood production in 2003 (fig. 2). Overall, the South's roundwood production increased 1.2 million cords to a total of 47.6 million cords (table A.4). At 33.2 million cords, softwood accounted for 70 percent of the total roundwood production. Softwood roundwood production was up 5 percent, or >1.5 million cords, while hardwood roundwood production declined >278,000 cords, or 2 percent. By comparison to the peak year of 1997, softwood roundwood production was down only 744,000 cords, or 2 percent, while hardwood round-wood production dropped 5.9 million cords, or 29 percent.

Only four Southern States—Arkansas, South Carolina, Tennessee, and Virginia—showed declines in roundwood production, ranging from 1 to 15 percent. Most Southern States showed small to moderate increases in roundwood production. Georgia's roundwood production increased 5 percent and led in total roundwood production with 8.2 million cords and was the leading producer of softwood roundwood at 6.9 million cords. Alabama's roundwood production increased 1 percent and was a very close second

to Georgia in total roundwood production with 7.9 million cords. Alabama was the leading producer of hardwood roundwood, at 2.7 million cords. Mississippi, Louisiana, and South Carolina followed with 5.4, 4.8, and 4.3 million cords, respectively. Combined production in these five States amounted to 30.7 million cords, or 64 percent of the South's roundwood total.

Wood Residues

Mills reported two types of receipts: (1) roundwood and (2) wood residues. Wood residues consist primarily of mill residue chips, a byproduct of sawmilling and veneer mill operations. Chips that are produced in the woods or generated when material received as roundwood by primary producers is chipped instead of being milled are not technically wood residues, but are reported as mill residues in this bulletin.

In 2007, wood residue production in the South declined 178,900 cords, or 1 percent, from 18.3 million cords in 2006 to 18.2 million cords, or 43.9 million tons (table A.5). Softwood residue production declined 1 percent to 14.1 million cords and accounted for 78 percent of wood residues produced. Hardwood residue production was down only 6,300 cords, remaining relatively stable at 4.0 million cords.

Eight Southern States showed a decline in wood residue production, while five States had moderate increases ranging from 3 to 14 percent. Alabama led Southern States in the production of wood residues at 2.8 million cords, followed by Georgia with 2.3 million cords and Mississippi, North Carolina, and Virginia with 2.0, 1.9, and 1.8 million cords, respectively. Combined wood residue production in these five States amounted to 10.7 million cords, or 59 percent of the South's total.

County or Parish Production

Table A.6 summarizes pulpwood production in the South by source of wood, State, year, and number of mills for the years 1996-2007. Tables A.7 through A.19 report county and parish (herein county) patterns of roundwood pulpwood production for domestic pulpmills. Wood residues and pulpwood production exported outside the U.S. are not included in these figures because the county of origin for the residues and exports are difficult, if not impossible, to determine. Of the 1,002 counties in the Southern States, 877 produced softwood or hardwood roundwood or both compared to 900 in 2006, 872 in 2005, and 873 in 2004. Of the producing counties, only 17, or 2 percent, harvested more than 250,000 cords of softwood and hardwood roundwood combined, with 11 of the 17 counties in Alabama and Louisiana. Sixteen percent, or 138 counties evenly distributed across the South, had roundwood pulpwood production ranging between 100,000 and 250,000 cords, while 175 counties had production that ranged between 50,000 and 99,999

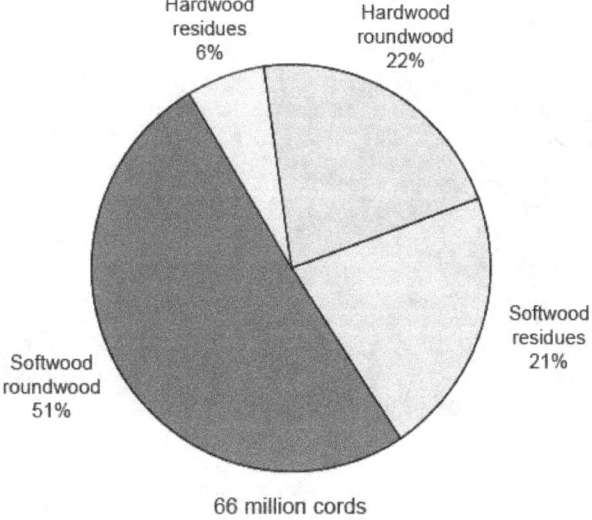

Figure 2—Softwood and hardwood components of Southern pulpwood production, 2007.

cords. The remaining 547 counties, or 62 percent of producing counties, had production of <50,000 cords. Figures 3 and 4 show production of softwood and hardwood roundwood pulpwood in cords per square mile, which discounts the effect of county size on concentration of production. In both figures, counties in yellow are those that produced >100 cords per square mile. Across the South, 333 counties had production of >100 cords of softwood per square mile, while only 92 counties had hardwood production in that range (table 1).

A barometer for degree of local competition for pulpwood is the number of mills procuring wood from each county (figs. 5 and 6). In 386 of the producing counties, or 44 percent, 1 to 3 mills were actively procuring both softwood and hardwood roundwood (table 2). In 339 counties, or 39 percent, 4 to 6 mills were actively procuring wood; and in the remaining 152 counties, or 17 percent, 7 or more mills were active. By comparison, in 1997 a peak year for Southern pulpwood production, there were 103 pulpmills active in the South (table A.6) and 347 counties, or 38 percent, had 7 or more mills competing for wood.

Table 1—Number of producing counties in the South, by range of cords per square mile for softwood and hardwood roundwood, 2007

Range	Softwood	Hardwood
cords/sq. mi.	number of counties	
0	55	24
0.001–10.0	191	212
10.1–50.0	166	346
50.1–100.0	132	203
100.1+	333	92
Total	877	877

Table 2—Number of producing counties in the South, by number of pulpmills procuring softwood and hardwood roundwood, 2007

Mills	Combined[a]	Softwood[b]	Hardwood[c]
number	number of counties		
0	0	55	244
1–3	386	298	408
4–6	339	284	203
7–9	118	66	20
10+	34	10	2
Total	877	877	877

[a] Combined is counties with mills procuring both softwood and hardwood.

[b] Softwood is counties with mills procuring only softwood.

[c] Hardwood is counties with mills procuring only hardwood.

Roundwood Movement

Tables A.20 and A.21 show the softwood and hardwood roundwood pulpwood movement for the Southeast and South Central regions. Numbers in boxes represent roundwood harvested and retained for processing within each State. The numbers in rows to the left and right of those boxed numbers represent wood exported to the other States. Therefore, the sum of the figure for retained wood and the figure for wood exported out of State is the total roundwood production for the State. The numbers in columns either above or below the figures for retained wood represent wood that was imported from other States. The sum of the retained figure and the figure for wood imported from other States represents roundwood receipts or the amount of roundwood processed by mills in a State.

The South Central region was a net importer of roundwood pulpwood. For both softwood and hardwood combined, imports exceeded exports by 479,388 cords (tables A.20 and A.21). Softwood imports exceeded exports by 138,981 cords, while hardwood imports exceeded exports by 340,407 cords. The Southeast was a net exporter of pulpwood with softwood and hardwood exports exceeding imports by 519,264 cords. Softwood exports exceeded imports by 343,549 cords, while hardwood exports exceeded imports by 175,715 cords. Pulpwood exports from the Southeast is greater than the pulpwood imports in the South Central region in part because of exports from the Southeast to mills in Maryland, Ohio, and Pennsylvania. Southwide, pulpwood production exceeded receipts or consumption by 39,876 cords.

Mills

In 2007, 87 southern pulpmills were operating and drawing wood from the 13 Southern States (fig. 7), the same as in 2006. At the same time, total southern mill pulping capacity increased from 125,093 tons per day in 2006 to 125,565 tons per day in 2007. Southern mills account for >70 percent of the Nation's total pulping capacity. Daily capacity of individual mills ranged from 50 tons to 3,600 tons. In 1992, average pulpmill capacity was 1,295 tons per day, increasing to 1,386 tons per day in 1999, and then dropping to 1,310 tons per day in 2001. The average daily capacity totaled 1,443 tons per day in 2007, slightly higher than in 2006 and in 2005. The sulfate process dominated the industry in 2007, accounting for 88 percent of mill capacity. Groundwood or other mechanical processes accounted for 6 percent, semichemical 5 percent, and soda and other chemical processes 1 percent (table A.22). These proportions have remained relatively stable over the past few years. Based on 2007 production and mill capacity, and using an average of 350 total operating days, southern pulpmills operated at 94-percent capacity.

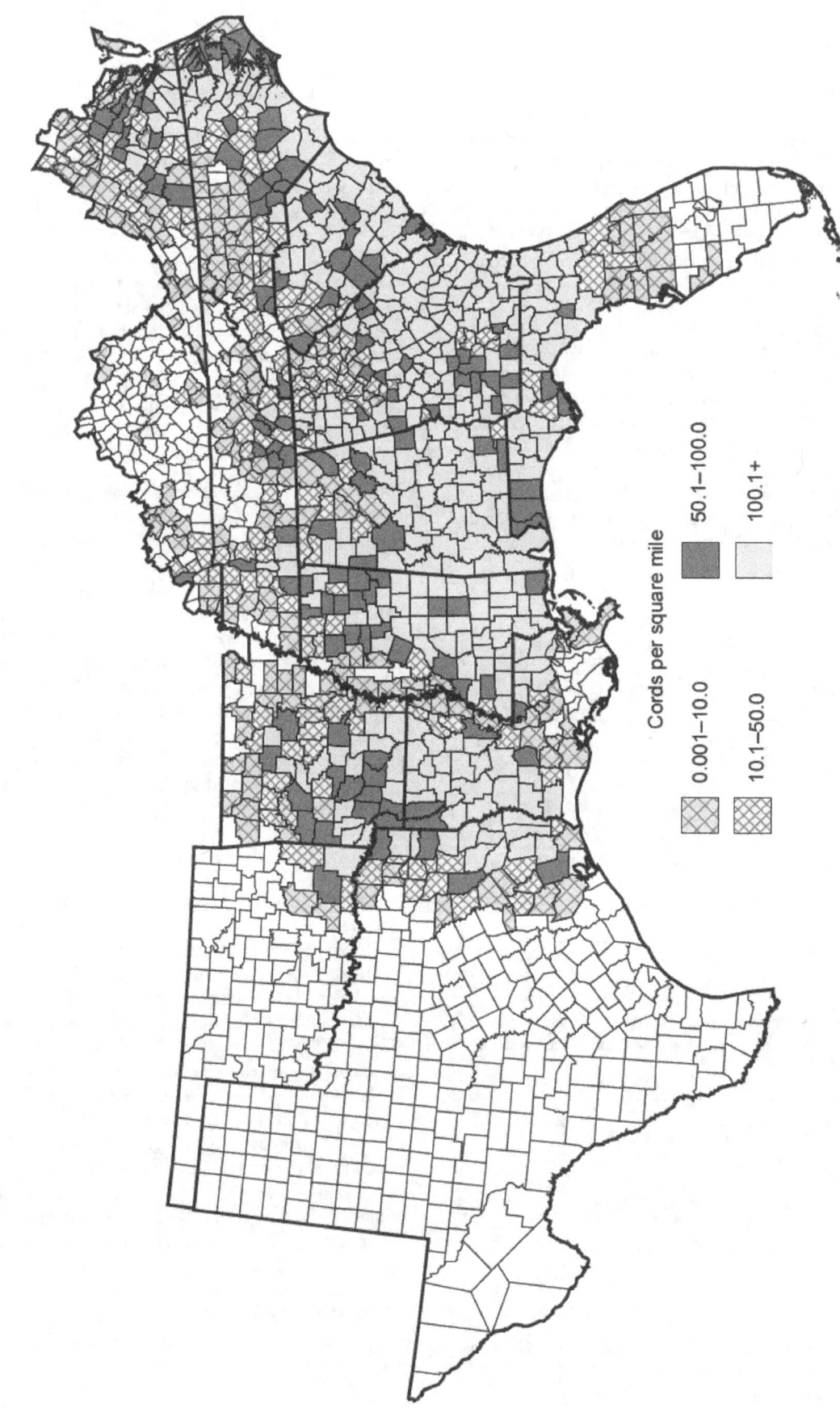

Figure 3—Softwood roundwood production in the South by county or parish, 2007.

Cords per square mile

0.001–10.0

10.1–50.0

50.1–100.0

100.1+

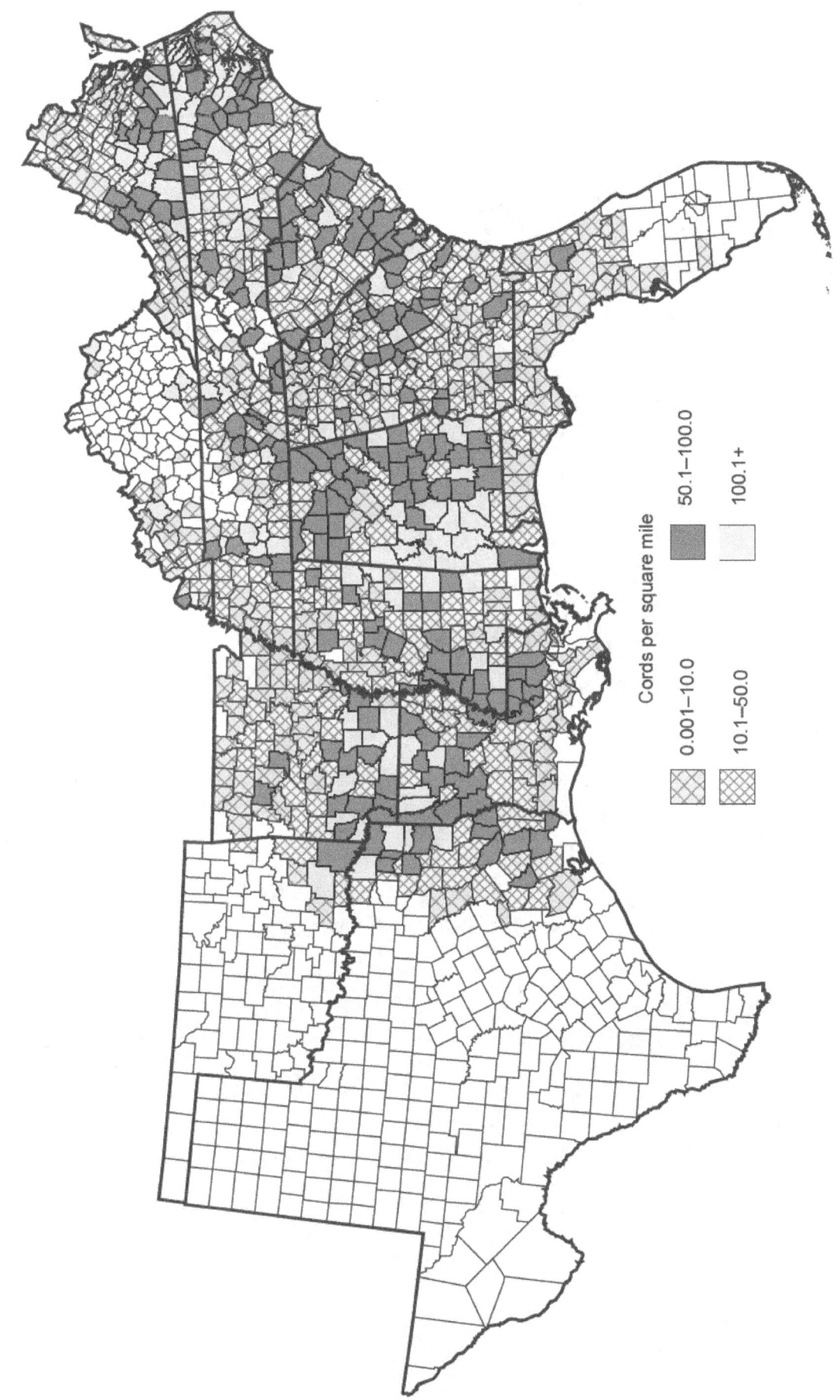

Figure 4—Hardwood roundwood production in the South by county or parish, 2007.

Cords per square mile

0.001–10.0

10.1–50.0

50.1–100.0

100.1+

5

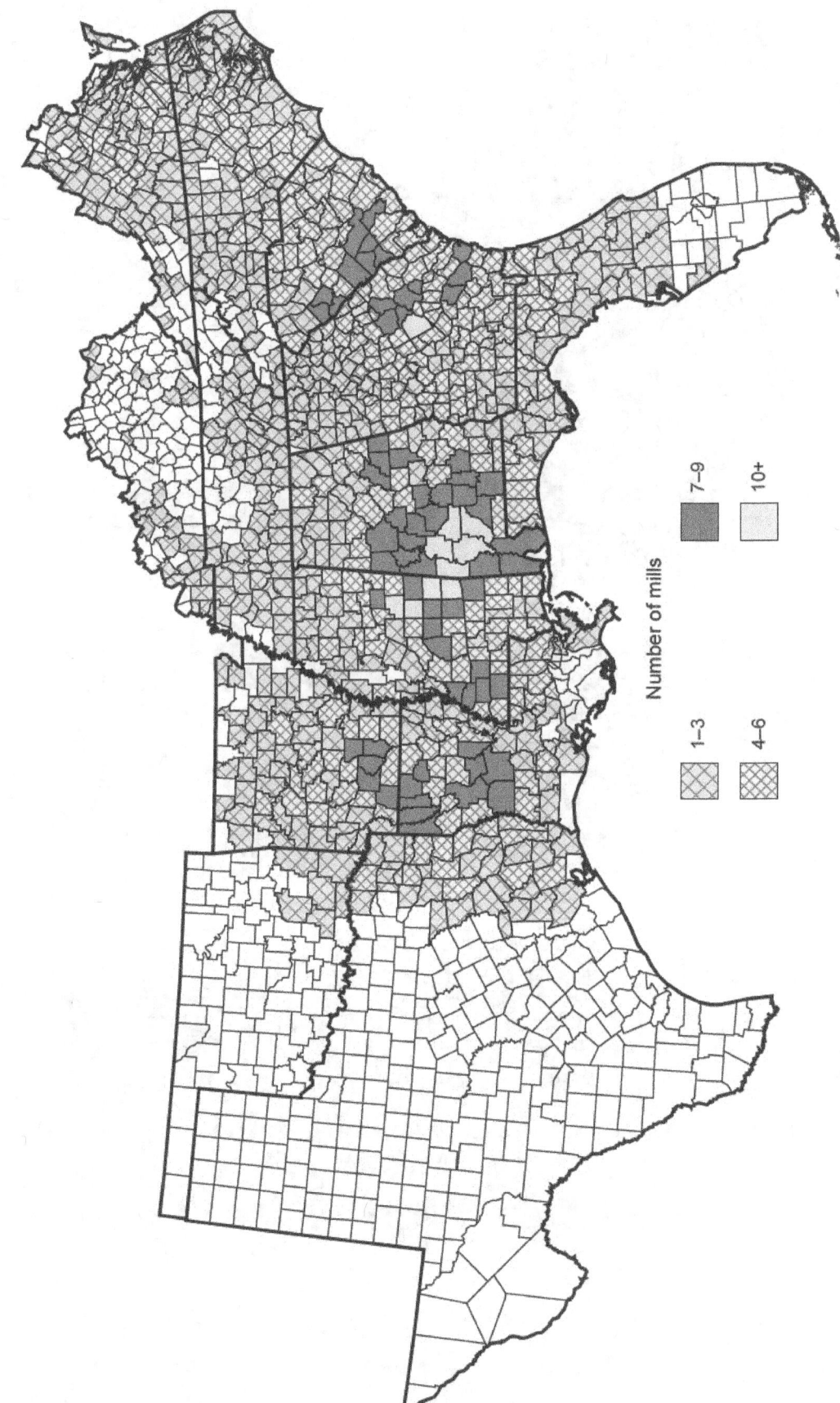

Figure 5—Number of mills competing for softwood roundwood by county or parish, 2007.

Number of mills

1–3

4–6

7–9

10+

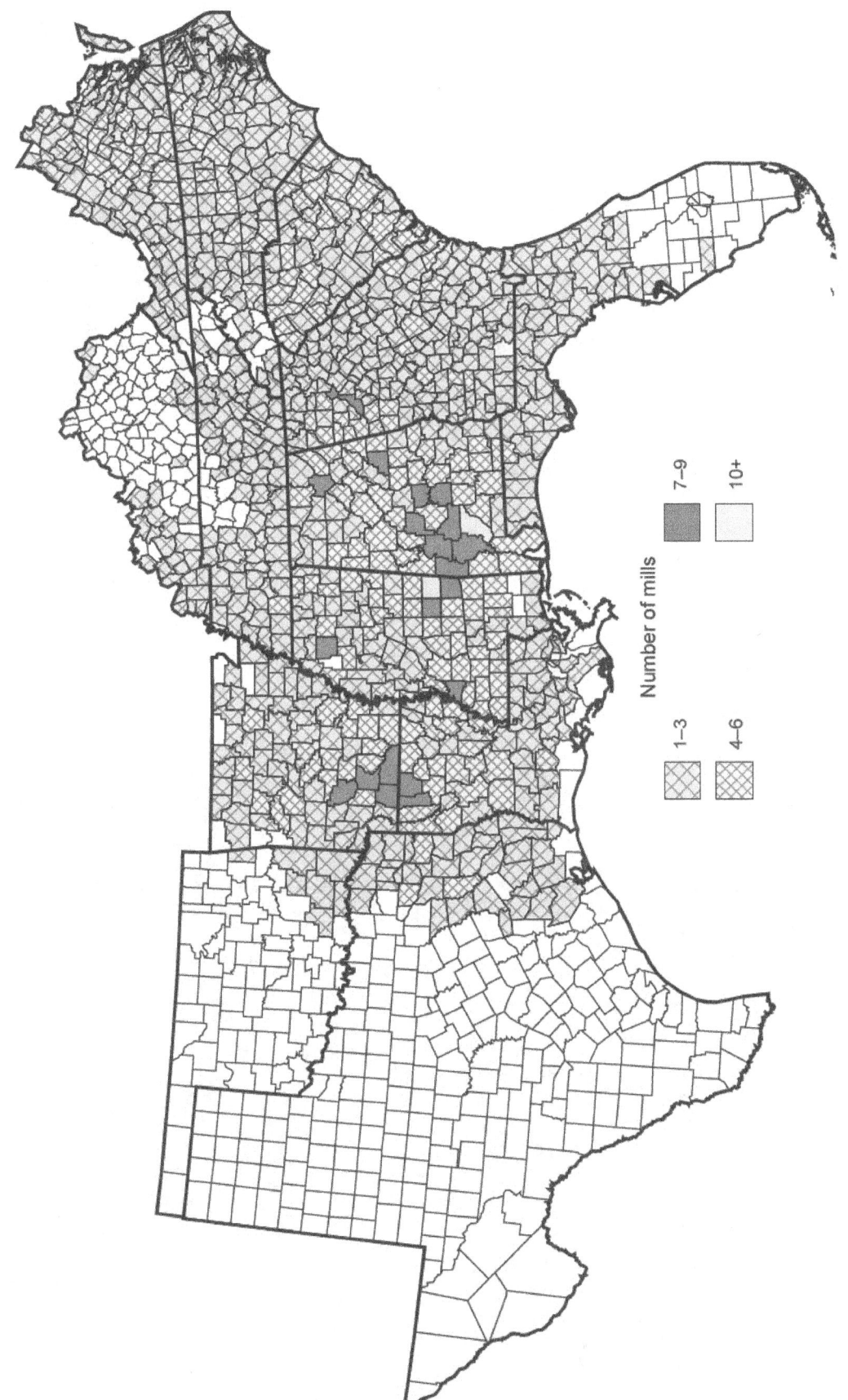

Figure 6—Number of mills competing for hardwood roundwood by county or parish, 2007.

Number of mills

1–3
4–6
7–9
10+

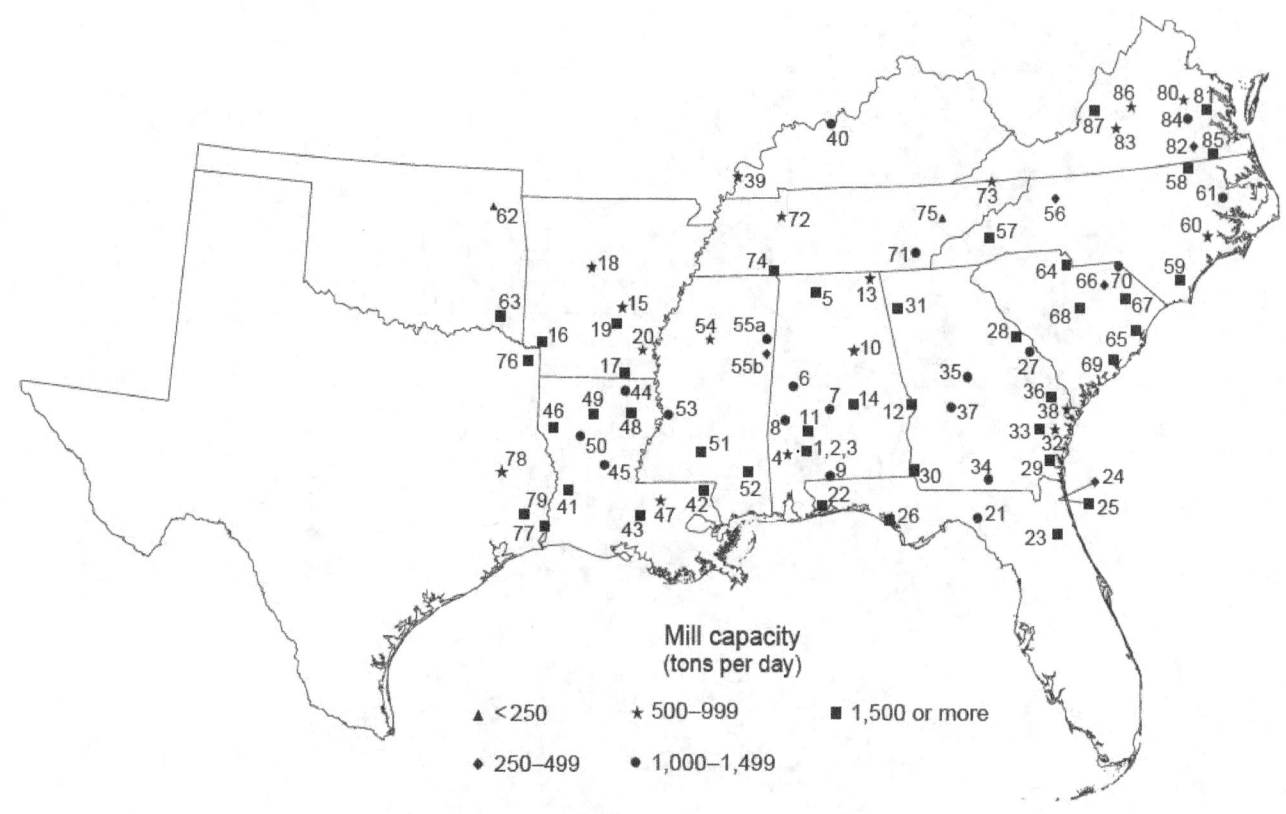

Figure 7—Capacity of southern pulpmills operating and drawing wood from the 13 Southern States, 2007. Numerals are coded on Table A.22.

Alabama and Georgia continued to lead the South in the number of mills operating with 14 and 12, respectively. Georgia led in pulping capacity with 21,015 tons per day, to Alabama's 20,080 tons per day (table 3). In addition, three pulpmills outside the southern region drew wood from the South in 2007 (table A.23).

Trends

From 1998 through 2007, southern pulpwood production declined by 12 percent, from 74.7 (197.3 million green tons) to 65.7 million cords (173.8 million green tons) (fig. 8). During the same period, roundwood pulpwood production declined from 52.7 to 47.6 million cords, a 10-percent loss. Between 1998 and 2007, softwood roundwood production declined 3 percent, while hardwood roundwood production declined 23 percent. The production of wood residues declined 17 percent from 21.9 million cords in 1998 to 18.2 million cords in 2007. Wood residues continue to be an important source of fiber for the pulp and paper industry in the South. Wood residues accounted for 28 percent of total pulpwood production in 2007, about the same as in 1998.

Table 3—Number of pulpmills and pulping capacity, by State, 2007

State	Mills	24-hour capacity
	number	tons
Alabama	14	20,080
Arkansas	6	7,750
Florida	6	8,580
Georgia	12	21,015
Kentucky	2	2,250
Louisiana	10	16,340
Mississippi	5	8,090
North Carolina	6	7,535
Oklahoma	2	2,850
South Carolina	7	10,550
Tennessee	5	4,875
Texas	4	5,846
Virginia	8	9,804
Total	87	125,565

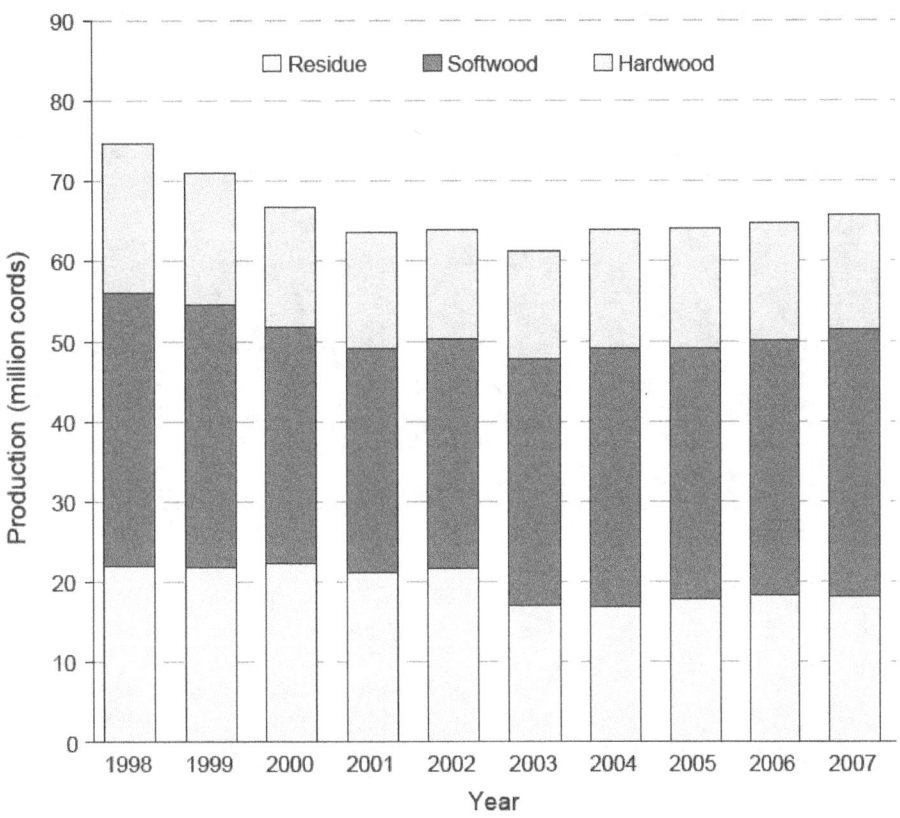

Figure 8—Southern pulpwood production, 1998–2007.

Appendix

Table A.1—Pulpwood production in the Southeast and South Central regions, 2007

Region and source of wood	All species	Softwood	Hardwood	All species	Softwood	Hardwood
		standard cords			*green tons*	
Southeast[a]						
Roundwood	21,711,365	16,460,680	5,250,685	59,145,755	44,443,837	14,701,918
Residues	8,659,123	6,366,335	2,292,788	20,962,757	15,311,035	5,651,722
Total	30,370,488	22,827,015	7,543,473	80,108,512	59,754,872	20,353,640
South Central[b]						
Roundwood	25,867,698	16,787,781	9,079,917	70,750,777	45,327,010	25,423,767
Residues	9,508,687	7,754,595	1,754,092	22,973,638	18,649,801	4,323,837
Total	35,376,385	24,542,376	10,834,009	93,724,415	63,976,811	29,747,604
Entire South						
Roundwood	47,579,063	33,248,461	14,330,602	129,896,532	89,770,847	40,125,685
Residues	18,167,810	14,120,930	4,046,880	43,936,395	33,960,836	9,975,559
Total	65,746,873	47,369,391	18,377,482	173,832,927	123,731,683	50,101,244

[a] States of Florida, Georgia, North Carolina, South Carolina, and Virginia.

[b] States of Alabama, Arkansas, Kentucky, Louisiana, Mississippi, Oklahoma, Tennessee, and Texas.

Table A.2—Pulpwood production in the South by State and species group, 2007

State	All species	Softwood	Hardwood
		standard cords	
Alabama	10,632,358	7,568,358	3,064,000
Arkansas	4,283,219	2,925,820	1,357,399
Florida	4,402,139	4,170,769	231,370
Georgia	10,549,979	8,787,069	1,762,910
Kentucky	640,766	59,135	581,631
Louisiana	6,469,287	5,241,292	1,227,995
Mississippi	7,393,751	5,534,291	1,859,460
North Carolina	5,564,663	3,247,453	2,317,210
Oklahoma	663,264	437,298	225,966
South Carolina	5,949,832	4,659,504	1,290,328
Tennessee	1,945,807	630,309	1,315,498
Texas	3,347,933	2,145,873	1,202,060
Virginia	3,903,875	1,962,220	1,941,655
All States	65,746,873	47,369,391	18,377,482

Table A.3—Pulpwood production in the South during 2007, and change since 2006

State	Change	Pulpwood	
	percent	*standard cords*	*green tons*
Alabama	1	10,632,358	28,185,165
Arkansas	-6	4,283,219	11,336,603
Florida	3	4,402,139	11,583,058
Georgia	3	10,549,979	27,959,109
Kentucky	-4	640,766	1,682,156
Louisiana	2	6,469,287	17,088,652
Mississippi	4	7,393,751	19,559,934
North Carolina	8	5,564,663	14,682,680
Oklahoma	2	663,264	1,752,835
South Carolina	-2	5,949,832	15,709,716
Tennessee	0	1,945,807	5,257,942
Texas	7	3,347,933	8,861,128
Virginia	-4	3,903,875	10,173,949
All States	2	65,746,873	173,832,927

Table A.4—Roundwood production in the South by State and species group, 2007 and 2006

State	Change from 2006	2007			2006		
		All species	Softwood	Hardwood	All species	Softwood	Hardwood
	percent	*thousand cords*					
Alabama	1	7,879.4	5,227.3	2,652.1	7,807.4	5,296.5	2,510.8
Arkansas	-1	3,068.2	1,845.5	1,222.7	3,090.9	1,785.1	1,305.8
Florida	7	3,300.8	3,093.4	207.4	3,082.2	2,847.4	234.8
Georgia	5	8,230.0	6,910.5	1,319.5	7,817.5	6,389.9	1,427.6
Kentucky	2	323.9	57.2	266.7	317.3	61.4	255.8
Louisiana	3	4,793.5	3,736.9	1,056.6	4,661.4	3,501.8	1,159.6
Mississippi	8	5,421.8	3,748.0	1,673.9	5,018.4	3,411.0	1,607.4
North Carolina	9	3,707.1	2,031.5	1,675.7	3,389.4	1,885.4	1,504.1
Oklahoma	4	459.6	245.7	213.9	439.8	261.6	178.3
South Carolina	-1	4,344.6	3,312.1	1,032.5	4,386.4	3,253.3	1,133.1
Tennessee	-1	1,561.9	597.6	964.3	1,578.1	579.1	999.0
Texas	4	2,359.4	1,329.6	1,029.8	2,259.0	1,236.8	1,022.2
Virginia	-15	2,128.8	1,113.2	1,015.7	2,490.7	1,220.5	1,270.3
All States	3	47,579.1	33,248.5	14,330.6	46,338.5	31,729.8	14,608.7

Numbers in rows and columns may not sum to totals due to rounding.

Table A.5—Southern output of wood residues for pulp manufacture by State and species group, 2007 and 2006

State	Change from 2006	2007			2006		
		All species	Softwood	Hardwood	All species	Softwood	Hardwood
	percent	*thousand cords*					
Alabama	3	2,753.0	2,341.0	411.9	2,673.2	2,119.8	553.4
Arkansas	-18	1,215.1	1,080.4	134.7	1,481.0	1,322.1	158.9
Florida	-8	1,101.3	1,077.4	24.0	1,197.1	1,162.1	35.0
Georgia	-4	2,320.0	1,876.5	443.4	2,420.9	1,950.3	470.6
Kentucky	-9	316.9	1.9	314.9	347.1	2.4	344.7
Louisiana	0	1,675.8	1,504.4	171.4	1,679.0	1,478.2	200.8
Mississippi	-4	1,971.9	1,786.3	185.6	2,063.3	1,857.5	205.8
North Carolina	4	1,857.5	1,216.0	641.5	1,786.7	1,195.1	591.6
Oklahoma	-4	203.7	191.6	12.1	212.2	202.2	10.0
South Carolina	-4	1,605.3	1,347.4	257.9	1,665.7	1,442.4	223.3
Tennessee	5	383.9	32.7	351.2	366.8	17.7	349.1
Texas	14	988.5	816.2	172.3	866.1	736.7	129.4
Virginia	12	1,775.0	849.0	926.0	1,587.6	807.1	780.5
All States	-1	18,167.8	14,120.9	4,046.9	18,346.7	14,293.5	4,053.2

Numbers in rows and columns may not sum to totals due to rounding.

Table A.6—Pulpwood production in the South by source of wood, State, year, and number of mills

Source of wood and State	Year											
	1996	1997	1998	1999	2000	2001	2002	2003	2004	2005	2006	2007
	thousand green tons											
Roundwood												
Alabama	26,791	27,814	29,344	23,685	21,537	20,575	21,537	19,222	20,535	20,913	21,331	21,540
Arkansas	8,755	8,416	8,908	10,362	8,009	7,582	7,720	7,751	9,134	8,551	8,476	8,406
Florida	10,632	10,610	10,807	9,641	9,802	9,619	9,397	10,096	9,250	7,950	8,345	8,933
Georgia	20,114	21,972	19,394	21,506	20,433	18,218	18,875	20,786	20,558	19,656	21,250	22,353
Kentucky	688	599	693	675	637	556	637	715	681	891	882	901
Louisiana	11,883	11,933	12,527	13,064	11,467	10,748	9,934	11,317	11,998	12,601	12,702	13,048
Mississippi	15,799	17,452	16,924	14,926	12,936	11,637	10,578	11,150	14,320	13,525	13,710	14,806
North Carolina	10,298	12,733	12,247	9,771	9,065	8,688	8,486	9,415	9,982	9,830	9,302	10,177
Oklahoma	1,484	1,610	2,060	1,818	1,272	1,118	1,669	1,466	1,216	1,214	1,206	1,262
South Carolina	11,466	12,305	11,702	12,340	10,501	10,284	10,416	10,706	11,769	12,256	11,957	11,834
Tennessee	4,188	4,479	4,345	4,463	4,891	4,685	4,284	4,463	4,098	4,458	4,361	4,314
Texas	6,347	10,585	7,314	6,019	4,195	5,843	5,720	7,124	7,327	7,179	6,202	6,473
Virginia	7,160	7,927	7,970	6,315	6,571	6,176	5,756	6,764	7,425	7,255	6,852	5,849
All States	135,605	148,435	144,235	134,585	121,316	115,729	115,009	120,974	128,292	126,280	126,575	129,897
Residues	45,887	52,468	53,095	52,900	53,898	51,340	52,603	41,039	40,711	42,982	44,367	43,936
Total	181,492	200,903	197,330	187,485	175,214	167,069	167,612	162,012	169,003	169,262	170,943	173,833
Number of mills	105	103	103	97	98	94	92	91	89	87	87	87

Numbers in columns may not sum to totals due to rounding.

Table A.7—Roundwood pulpwood production in Alabama, 2007

County[a]	All species	Softwood	Hardwood	All species	Softwood	Hardwood
	standard cords			green tons		
Autauga	88,033	52,501	35,532	241,243	141,753	99,490
Baldwin	197,583	170,684	26,899	536,164	460,847	75,317
Barbour	209,343	151,854	57,489	570,975	410,006	160,969
Bibb	123,838	50,440	73,398	341,702	136,188	205,514
Blount	32,087	2,307	29,780	89,613	6,229	83,384
Bullock	145,207	120,365	24,842	394,544	324,986	69,558
Butler	192,018	155,765	36,253	522,074	420,566	101,508
Calhoun	48,207	38,723	9,484	131,107	104,552	26,555
Chambers	49,135	27,731	21,404	134,805	74,874	59,931
Cherokee	117,044	88,901	28,143	318,833	240,033	78,800
Chilton	74,907	50,147	24,760	204,725	135,397	69,328
Choctaw	337,495	213,644	123,851	923,622	576,839	346,783
Clarke	522,040	323,595	198,445	1,429,353	873,707	555,646
Clay	128,239	99,040	29,199	349,165	267,408	81,757
Cleburne	111,802	88,658	23,144	304,180	239,377	64,803
Coffee	78,600	50,059	28,541	215,074	135,159	79,915
Colbert	35,531	17,303	18,228	97,756	46,718	51,038
Conecuh	289,402	224,261	65,141	787,900	605,505	182,395
Coosa	154,930	124,716	30,214	421,332	336,733	84,599
Covington	213,188	174,594	38,594	579,467	471,404	108,063
Crenshaw	150,092	107,310	42,782	409,527	289,737	119,790
Cullman	26,704	2,521	24,183	74,519	6,807	67,712
Dale	54,209	21,809	32,400	149,604	58,884	90,720
Dallas	195,931	122,574	73,357	536,350	330,950	205,400
De Kalb	64,600	33,027	31,573	177,577	89,173	88,404
Elmore	63,022	42,401	20,621	172,222	114,483	57,739
Escambia	132,744	106,264	26,480	361,057	286,913	74,144
Etowah	37,672	14,406	23,266	104,041	38,896	65,145
Fayette	59,511	44,772	14,739	162,153	120,884	41,269
Franklin	98,261	59,513	38,748	269,179	160,685	108,494
Geneva	29,044	24,952	4,092	78,828	67,370	11,458
Greene	95,365	49,464	45,901	262,076	133,553	128,523
Hale	141,803	95,552	46,251	387,493	257,990	129,503
Henry	106,458	67,138	39,320	291,369	181,273	110,096
Houston	24,053	18,431	5,622	65,506	49,764	15,742
Jackson	62,219	4,662	57,557	173,747	12,587	161,160
Jefferson	6,470	2,611	3,859	17,855	7,050	10,805
Lamar	50,672	31,953	18,719	138,686	86,273	52,413
Lauderdale	43,440	13,724	29,716	120,260	37,055	83,205
Lawrence	47,721	22,275	25,446	131,392	60,143	71,249
Lee	52,098	40,557	11,541	141,819	109,504	32,315
Limestone	10,026	2,409	7,617	27,832	6,504	21,328
Lowndes	107,387	77,096	30,291	292,974	208,159	84,815
Macon	122,478	98,496	23,982	333,089	265,939	67,150
Madison	26,048	9,118	16,930	72,023	24,619	47,404
Marengo	324,557	198,417	126,140	888,918	535,726	353,192

continued

Table A.7—Roundwood pulpwood production in Alabama, 2007 (continued)

County[a]	All species	Softwood	Hardwood	All species	Softwood	Hardwood
	standard cords			green tons		
Marion	98,152	68,098	30,054	268,016	183,865	84,151
Marshall	17,172	1,704	15,468	47,911	4,601	43,310
Mobile	169,506	103,621	65,885	464,255	279,777	184,478
Monroe	269,018	175,578	93,440	735,693	474,061	261,632
Montgomery	78,204	55,069	23,135	213,464	148,686	64,778
Morgan	24,001	4,606	19,395	66,742	12,436	54,306
Perry	116,236	71,820	44,416	318,279	193,914	124,365
Pickens	169,268	90,831	78,437	464,868	245,244	219,624
Pike	96,352	68,362	27,990	262,949	184,577	78,372
Randolph	122,599	61,684	60,915	337,109	166,547	170,562
Russell	114,796	96,459	18,337	311,783	260,439	51,344
St. Clair	58,914	28,666	30,248	162,092	77,398	84,694
Shelby	80,547	59,757	20,790	219,556	161,344	58,212
Sumter	186,903	110,562	76,341	512,272	298,517	213,755
Talladega	83,889	70,717	13,172	227,818	190,936	36,882
Tallapoosa	140,347	95,298	45,049	383,442	257,305	126,137
Tuscaloosa	77,757	45,693	32,064	213,150	123,371	89,779
Walker	14,111	10,958	3,153	38,415	29,587	8,828
Washington	257,122	163,660	93,462	703,576	441,882	261,694
Wilcox	346,890	250,978	95,912	946,195	677,641	268,554
Winston	76,398	56,477	19,921	208,267	152,488	55,779
All counties	7,879,396	5,227,338	2,652,058	21,539,582	14,113,818	7,425,764

[a] Counties with no pulpwood production are omitted.

Table A.8—Roundwood pulpwood production in Arkansas, 2007

County[a]	All species	Softwood	Hardwood	All species	Softwood	Hardwood
		standard cords			green tons	
Arkansas	19,322	9,022	10,300	53,199	24,359	28,840
Ashley	266,136	177,002	89,134	727,480	477,905	249,575
Baxter	2,011	0	2,011	5,631	0	5,631
Boone	287	0	287	804	0	804
Bradley	136,648	72,509	64,139	375,363	195,774	179,589
Calhoun	57,049	21,483	35,566	157,589	58,004	99,585
Carroll	21	11	10	58	30	28
Chicot	8,041	5,675	2,366	21,948	15,323	6,625
Clark	159,604	47,997	111,607	442,092	129,592	312,500
Clay	49	49	0	132	132	0
Cleburne	47,521	36,708	10,813	129,388	99,112	30,276
Cleveland	90,835	52,227	38,608	249,115	141,013	108,102
Columbia	81,985	50,222	31,763	224,535	135,599	88,936
Conway	65,393	39,054	26,339	179,195	105,446	73,749
Crittenden	1,716	0	1,716	4,805	0	4,805
Cross	2,266	176	2,090	6,327	475	5,852
Dallas	88,839	55,646	33,193	243,184	150,244	92,940
Desha	28,539	112	28,427	79,898	302	79,596
Drew	182,771	146,151	36,620	497,144	394,608	102,536
Faulkner	11,298	8,421	2,877	30,793	22,737	8,056
Franklin	5,712	4,423	1,289	15,551	11,942	3,609
Garland	15,695	12,122	3,573	42,733	32,729	10,004
Grant	116,978	86,576	30,402	318,881	233,755	85,126
Greene	4,069	3,901	168	11,003	10,533	470
Hempstead	73,608	42,445	31,163	201,858	114,602	87,256
Hot Spring	44,553	37,716	6,837	120,977	101,833	19,144
Howard	127,528	78,436	49,092	349,235	211,777	137,458
Independence	33,040	9,644	23,396	91,548	26,039	65,509
Izard	449	56	393	1,251	151	1,100
Jackson	696	270	426	1,922	729	1,193
Jefferson	43,198	30,147	13,051	117,940	81,397	36,543
Johnson	33,404	10,482	22,922	92,483	28,301	64,182
Lafayette	50,743	24,831	25,912	139,598	67,044	72,554
Lawrence	6,586	0	6,586	18,441	0	18,441
Lee	1,860	0	1,860	5,208	0	5,208
Lincoln	66,407	15,305	51,102	184,410	41,324	143,086
Little River	83,646	41,372	42,274	230,071	111,704	118,367
Logan	13,301	11,518	1,783	36,091	31,099	4,992
Lonoke	10,702	9,446	1,256	29,021	25,504	3,517
Madison	3,178	20	3,158	8,896	54	8,842
Marion	1,467	75	1,392	4,101	203	3,898
Miller	61,403	26,003	35,400	169,328	70,208	99,120
Mississippi	451	0	451	1,263	0	1,263
Monroe	10,947	5,462	5,485	30,105	14,747	15,358
Montgomery	9,937	4,772	5,165	27,346	12,884	14,462
Nevada	56,668	38,463	18,205	154,824	103,850	50,974

continued

Table A.8—Roundwood pulpwood production in Arkansas, 2007 (continued)

County[a]	All species	Softwood	Hardwood	All species	Softwood	Hardwood
	standard cords			*green tons*		
Newton	2,530	18	2,512	7,083	49	7,034
Ouachita	54,018	33,168	20,850	147,934	89,554	58,380
Perry	71,203	65,611	5,592	192,808	177,150	15,658
Phillips	7,069	3,445	3,624	19,449	9,302	10,147
Pike	119,739	99,289	20,450	325,340	268,080	57,260
Poinsett	961	144	817	2,677	389	2,288
Polk	55,202	41,478	13,724	150,418	111,991	38,427
Pope	17,884	12,918	4,966	48,784	34,879	13,905
Prairie	16,113	13,416	2,697	43,775	36,223	7,552
Pulaski	10,683	6,703	3,980	29,242	18,098	11,144
Randolph	63	0	63	176	0	176
St. Francis	14,886	355	14,531	41,646	959	40,687
Saline	57,066	49,319	7,747	154,853	133,161	21,692
Scott	48,840	33,691	15,149	133,383	90,966	42,417
Searcy	15,797	1,198	14,599	44,112	3,235	40,877
Sebastian	167	167	0	451	451	0
Sevier	84,304	60,352	23,952	230,016	162,950	67,066
Sharp	1,426	230	1,196	3,970	621	3,349
Stone	11,894	5,068	6,826	32,797	13,684	19,113
Union	185,959	95,072	90,887	511,178	256,694	254,484
Van Buren	47,184	27,652	19,532	129,350	74,660	54,690
Washington	22	11	11	61	30	31
White	53,515	40,516	12,999	145,790	109,393	36,397
Woodruff	2,600	1,615	985	7,119	4,361	2,758
Yell	62,483	38,079	24,404	171,144	102,813	68,331
All counties	3,068,165	1,845,465	1,222,700	8,406,321	4,982,757	3,423,564

[a] Counties with no pulpwood production are omitted.

Table A.9—Roundwood pulpwood production in Florida, 2007

County[a]	All species	Softwood	Hardwood	All species	Softwood	Hardwood
	standard cords			*green tons*		
Alachua	69,882	66,419	3,463	189,027	179,331	9,696
Baker	133,585	129,013	4,572	361,137	348,335	12,802
Bay	168,650	155,981	12,669	456,622	421,149	35,473
Bradford	89,478	83,459	6,019	242,192	225,339	16,853
Brevard	1,478	1,478	0	3,991	3,991	0
Calhoun	96,625	90,536	6,089	261,496	244,447	17,049
Charlotte	230	210	20	623	567	56
Citrus	983	934	49	2,659	2,522	137
Clay	100,814	97,471	3,343	272,532	263,172	9,360
Columbia	145,603	138,245	7,358	393,864	373,262	20,602
Dixie	79,928	78,455	1,473	215,953	211,829	4,124
Duval	69,539	65,819	3,720	188,127	177,711	10,416
Escambia	42,323	37,333	4,990	114,771	100,799	13,972
Flagler	60,452	49,917	10,535	164,274	134,776	29,498
Franklin	21,141	20,851	290	57,110	56,298	812
Gadsden	55,330	40,252	15,078	150,898	108,680	42,218
Gilchrist	14,636	14,429	207	39,538	38,958	580
Gulf	138,631	131,580	7,051	375,009	355,266	19,743
Hamilton	126,832	124,421	2,411	342,688	335,937	6,751
Hernando	625	609	16	1,689	1,644	45
Hillsborough	465	49	416	1,297	132	1,165
Holmes	43,625	41,061	2,564	118,044	110,865	7,179
Jackson	117,128	108,845	8,283	317,074	293,882	23,192
Jefferson	77,447	76,130	1,317	209,239	205,551	3,688
Lafayette	145,840	144,631	1,209	393,889	390,504	3,385
Lake	17,387	10,325	7,062	47,652	27,878	19,774
Leon	18,146	16,110	2,036	49,198	43,497	5,701
Levy	113,445	107,753	5,692	306,871	290,933	15,938
Liberty	12,289	9,456	2,833	33,463	25,531	7,932
Madison	145,527	136,210	9,317	393,855	367,767	26,088
Marion	39,138	37,528	1,610	105,834	101,326	4,508
Nassau	173,900	162,667	11,233	470,653	439,201	31,452
Okaloosa	43,745	39,527	4,218	118,533	106,723	11,810
Orange	1,342	855	487	3,673	2,309	1,364
Osceola	8	8	0	22	22	0
Pasco	2,610	1,077	1,533	7,200	2,908	4,292
Polk	682	682	0	1,841	1,841	0
Putnam	149,497	123,162	26,335	406,275	332,537	73,738
St. ohns J	58,160	51,196	6,964	157,728	138,229	19,499
Santa Rosa	55,126	53,052	2,074	149,047	143,240	5,807
Sarasota	5	5	0	14	14	0
Seminole	366	340	26	991	918	73
Sumter	1,063	23	1,040	2,974	62	2,912
Suwannee	86,924	79,324	7,600	235,455	214,175	21,280
Taylor	227,903	226,280	1,623	615,500	610,956	4,544
Union	18,469	17,701	768	49,943	47,793	2,150

continued

Table A.9—Roundwood pulpwood production in Florida, 2007 (continued)

County[a]	All species	Softwood	Hardwood	All species	Softwood	Hardwood
	standard cords			*green tons*		
Volusia	21,043	18,375	2,668	57,083	49,613	7,470
Wakulla	37,788	37,683	105	102,038	101,744	294
Walton	138,362	136,252	2,110	373,788	367,880	5,908
Washington	136,603	129,676	6,927	369,521	350,125	19,396
All counties	3,300,798	3,093,395	207,403	8,932,895	8,352,169	580,726

[a] Counties with no pulpwood production are omitted.

Table A.10—Roundwood pulpwood production in Georgia, 2007

County[a]	All species	Softwood	Hardwood	All species	Softwood	Hardwood
	standard cords			*green tons*		
Appling	150,512	135,610	14,902	407,873	366,147	41,726
Atkinson	39,523	29,663	9,860	107,698	80,090	27,608
Bacon	88,493	82,245	6,248	239,556	222,062	17,494
Baker	24,644	23,117	1,527	66,692	62,416	4,276
Baldwin	26,976	19,034	7,942	73,630	51,392	22,238
Banks	7,791	3,036	4,755	21,511	8,197	13,314
Barrow	2,422	1,163	1,259	6,665	3,140	3,525
Bartow	71,111	63,316	7,795	192,779	170,953	21,826
Ben Hill	3,023	2,564	459	8,208	6,923	1,285
Berrien	20,378	12,891	7,487	55,770	34,806	20,964
Bibb	28,108	15,021	13,087	77,201	40,557	36,644
Bleckley	42,273	38,136	4,137	114,551	102,967	11,584
Brantley	159,621	156,663	2,958	431,272	422,990	8,282
Brooks	27,695	27,695	0	74,777	74,777	0
Bryan	53,261	43,843	9,418	144,746	118,376	26,370
Bulloch	83,593	67,552	16,041	227,305	182,390	44,915
Burke	213,260	156,678	56,582	581,461	423,031	158,430
Butts	8,445	8,089	356	22,837	21,840	997
Calhoun	26,349	24,689	1,660	71,308	66,660	4,648
Camden	206,244	198,712	7,532	557,612	536,522	21,090
Candler	56,674	51,942	4,732	153,493	140,243	13,250
Carroll	42,028	40,554	1,474	113,623	109,496	4,127
Catoosa	10,883	6,186	4,697	29,854	16,702	13,152
Charlton	268,240	265,019	3,221	724,570	715,551	9,019
Chatham	38,307	24,547	13,760	104,805	66,277	38,528
Chattahoochee	18,150	12,378	5,772	49,583	33,421	16,162
Chattooga	30,210	27,759	2,451	81,812	74,949	6,863
Cherokee	43,428	34,472	8,956	118,151	93,074	25,077
Clarke	203	131	72	556	354	202
Clay	52,192	49,300	2,892	141,208	133,110	8,098
Clayton	503	349	154	1,373	942	431
Clinch	136,706	104,794	31,912	372,298	282,944	89,354
Cobb	2,462	2,354	108	6,658	6,356	302
Coffee	52,822	49,027	3,795	142,999	132,373	10,626
Colquitt	38,815	36,709	2,106	105,011	99,114	5,897
Columbia	17,361	10,836	6,525	47,527	29,257	18,270
Cook	7,883	5,646	2,237	21,508	15,244	6,264
Coweta	37,621	34,278	3,343	101,911	92,551	9,360
Crawford	67,927	63,047	4,880	183,891	170,227	13,664
Crisp	19,990	16,531	3,459	54,319	44,634	9,685
Dade	1,058	0	1,058	2,962	0	2,962
Dawson	6,695	6,523	172	18,094	17,612	482
Decatur	61,927	55,968	5,959	167,799	151,114	16,685
De Kalb	4,906	4,580	326	13,279	12,366	913
Dodge	112,953	97,912	15,041	306,477	264,362	42,115
Dooly	51,080	44,264	6,816	138,598	119,513	19,085

continued

Table A.10—Roundwood pulpwood production in Georgia, 2007 (continued)

County[a]	All species	Softwood	Hardwood	All species	Softwood	Hardwood
	standard cords			*green tons*		
Dougherty	19,905	14,602	5,303	54,273	39,425	14,848
Douglas	8,548	6,969	1,579	23,237	18,816	4,421
Early	49,201	42,692	6,509	133,493	115,268	18,225
Echols	42,161	38,606	3,555	114,190	104,236	9,954
Effingham	147,380	101,977	45,403	402,466	275,338	127,128
Elbert	14,043	1,995	12,048	39,121	5,387	33,734
Emanuel	181,984	164,311	17,673	493,124	443,640	49,484
Evans	36,008	32,846	3,162	97,538	88,684	8,854
Fannin	7,027	5,067	1,960	19,169	13,681	5,488
Fayette	1,159	525	634	3,193	1,418	1,775
Floyd	86,294	50,789	35,505	236,544	137,130	99,414
Forsyth	6,464	2,863	3,601	17,813	7,730	10,083
Franklin	11,018	185	10,833	30,832	500	30,332
Fulton	8,423	4,188	4,235	23,166	11,308	11,858
Gilmer	9,855	7,402	2,453	26,853	19,985	6,868
Glascock	18,218	12,420	5,798	49,768	33,534	16,234
Glynn	84,929	82,801	2,128	229,521	223,563	5,958
Gordon	45,275	40,279	4,996	122,742	108,753	13,989
Grady	49,797	25,119	24,678	136,919	67,821	69,098
Greene	23,783	16,302	7,481	64,962	44,015	20,947
Gwinnett	13,937	9,175	4,762	38,107	24,773	13,334
Habersham	27,839	17,961	9,878	76,153	48,495	27,658
Hall	8,353	4,713	3,640	22,917	12,725	10,192
Hancock	75,301	65,710	9,591	204,272	177,417	26,855
Haralson	41,916	35,978	5,938	113,767	97,141	16,626
Harris	65,533	54,734	10,799	178,019	147,782	30,237
Hart	7,738	4,979	2,759	21,168	13,443	7,725
Heard	47,698	46,902	796	128,864	126,635	2,229
Henry	12,412	5,864	6,548	34,167	15,833	18,334
Houston	39,396	32,359	7,037	107,073	87,369	19,704
Irwin	8,286	3,985	4,301	22,803	10,760	12,043
Jackson	15,650	3,023	12,627	43,518	8,162	35,356
Jasper	52,009	40,076	11,933	141,617	108,205	33,412
Jeff Davis	86,613	76,924	9,689	234,824	207,695	27,129
Jefferson	90,418	81,319	9,099	245,038	219,561	25,477
Jenkins	120,543	105,697	14,846	326,951	285,382	41,569
Johnson	68,745	53,332	15,413	187,152	143,996	43,156
Jones	83,853	69,475	14,378	227,841	187,583	40,258
Lamar	21,718	5,688	16,030	60,242	15,358	44,884
Lanier	10,639	9,801	838	28,809	26,463	2,346
Laurens	161,726	130,343	31,383	439,798	351,926	87,872
Lee	23,756	17,797	5,959	64,737	48,052	16,685
Liberty	82,468	65,531	16,937	224,358	176,934	47,424
Lincoln	28,670	22,139	6,531	78,062	59,775	18,287
Long	133,009	123,084	9,925	360,117	332,327	27,790
Lowndes	54,086	49,193	4,893	146,521	132,821	13,700

continued

Table A.10—Roundwood pulpwood production in Georgia, 2007 (continued)

County[a]	All species	Softwood	Hardwood	All species	Softwood	Hardwood
	standard cords			*green tons*		
Lumpkin	8,496	8,214	282	22,968	22,178	790
Macon	59,649	52,203	7,446	161,797	140,948	20,849
Madison	45,424	6,437	38,987	126,544	17,380	109,164
Marion	75,482	67,668	7,814	204,583	182,704	21,879
McDuffie	14,715	11,335	3,380	40,069	30,605	9,464
McIntosh	192,147	181,792	10,355	519,832	490,838	28,994
Meriwether	42,104	32,338	9,766	114,658	87,313	27,345
Miller	15,946	12,509	3,437	43,398	33,774	9,624
Mitchell	23,157	22,521	636	62,588	60,807	1,781
Monroe	62,541	51,352	11,189	169,979	138,650	31,329
Montgomery	72,926	63,533	9,393	197,839	171,539	26,300
Morgan	16,564	6,097	10,467	45,770	16,462	29,308
Murray	46,021	27,270	18,751	126,132	73,629	52,503
Muscogee	4,627	2,474	2,153	12,708	6,680	6,028
Newton	14,806	10,824	3,982	40,375	29,225	11,150
Oconee	2,129	384	1,745	5,923	1,037	4,886
Oglethorpe	6,978	3,145	3,833	19,224	8,492	10,732
Paulding	64,495	50,371	14,124	175,549	136,002	39,547
Peach	14,519	13,899	620	39,263	37,527	1,736
Pickens	33,332	30,679	2,653	90,261	82,833	7,428
Pierce	64,256	50,748	13,508	174,842	137,020	37,822
Pike	8,928	8,247	681	24,174	22,267	1,907
Polk	45,033	39,130	5,903	122,179	105,651	16,528
Pulaski	31,450	27,217	4,233	85,338	73,486	11,852
Putnam	33,982	25,364	8,618	92,613	68,483	24,130
Quitman	31,642	29,901	1,741	85,608	80,733	4,875
Rabun	2,274	1,203	1,071	6,247	3,248	2,999
Randolph	125,269	115,038	10,231	339,250	310,603	28,647
Richmond	47,976	37,136	10,840	130,619	100,267	30,352
Rockdale	1,201	1,198	3	3,243	3,235	8
Schley	48,974	48,633	341	132,264	131,309	955
Screven	182,171	150,703	31,468	495,008	406,898	88,110
Seminole	8,216	7,331	885	22,272	19,794	2,478
Spalding	2,102	1,773	329	5,708	4,787	921
Stephens	5,368	1,605	3,763	14,870	4,334	10,536
Stewart	122,961	106,465	16,496	333,645	287,456	46,189
Sumter	109,113	104,659	4,454	295,050	282,579	12,471
Talbot	93,377	77,314	16,063	253,724	208,748	44,976
Taliaferro	20,436	17,475	2,961	55,474	47,183	8,291
Tattnall	91,449	83,786	7,663	247,678	226,222	21,456
Taylor	84,311	75,441	8,870	228,527	203,691	24,836
Telfair	60,915	51,281	9,634	165,434	138,459	26,975
Terrell	43,776	42,264	1,512	118,347	114,113	4,234
Thomas	59,300	57,502	1,798	160,289	155,255	5,034
Tift	5,891	1,235	4,656	16,372	3,335	13,037
Toombs	146,894	132,831	14,063	398,020	358,644	39,376

continued

Table A.10—Roundwood pulpwood production in Georgia, 2007 (continued)

County[a]	All species	Softwood	Hardwood	All species	Softwood	Hardwood
	standard cords			*green tons*		
Towns	1,694	972	722	4,646	2,624	2,022
Treutlen	63,381	55,674	7,707	171,900	150,320	21,580
Troup	56,707	23,331	33,376	156,447	62,994	93,453
Turner	13,367	11,167	2,200	36,311	30,151	6,160
Twiggs	67,164	52,547	14,617	182,805	141,877	40,928
Union	10,033	8,363	1,670	27,256	22,580	4,676
Upson	56,562	48,286	8,276	153,545	130,372	23,173
Walker	20,016	13,638	6,378	54,681	36,823	17,858
Walton	2,010	644	1,366	5,564	1,739	3,825
Ware	238,101	225,549	12,552	644,128	608,982	35,146
Warren	48,064	38,151	9,913	130,764	103,008	27,756
Washington	112,780	84,006	28,774	307,383	226,816	80,567
Wayne	168,245	151,072	17,173	455,978	407,894	48,084
Webster	71,483	59,603	11,880	194,192	160,928	33,264
Wheeler	43,129	36,267	6,862	117,135	97,921	19,214
White	696	654	42	1,884	1,766	118
Whitfield	46,195	38,215	7,980	125,525	103,181	22,344
Wilcox	31,831	26,812	5,019	86,445	72,392	14,053
Wilkes	45,653	32,576	13,077	124,571	87,955	36,616
Wilkinson	109,279	78,722	30,557	298,109	212,549	85,560
Worth	31,774	31,218	556	85,846	84,289	1,557
All counties	8,230,017	6,910,535	1,319,482	22,353,000	18,658,451	3,694,549

[a] Counties with no pulpwood production are omitted.

Table A.11—Roundwood pulpwood production in Kentucky, 2007

County[a]	All species	Softwood	Hardwood	All species	Softwood	Hardwood
	standard cords			*green tons*		
Anderson	11	11	0	30	30	0
Ballard	9,832	0	9,832	27,530	0	27,530
Breckinridge	18,295	0	18,295	51,226	0	51,226
Caldwell	7,743	0	7,743	21,680	0	21,680
Calloway	7,350	5,524	1,826	20,028	14,915	5,113
Carlisle	13,779	10	13,769	38,580	27	38,553
Christian	8,864	8,054	810	24,014	21,746	2,268
Crittenden	12,479	6,574	5,905	34,284	17,750	16,534
Daviess	332	170	162	913	459	454
Fulton	954	11	943	2,670	30	2,640
Graves	5,205	225	4,980	14,552	608	13,944
Grayson	2,502	14	2,488	7,004	38	6,966
Greenup	42,320	477	41,843	118,448	1,288	117,160
Hancock	41	41	0	111	111	0
Hickman	1,484	181	1,303	4,137	489	3,648
Hopkins	3,188	585	2,603	8,868	1,580	7,288
Knox	29,723	73	29,650	83,217	197	83,020
Laurel	58,423	3,367	55,056	163,248	9,091	154,157
Lee	28	28	0	76	76	0
Lewis	235	168	67	642	454	188
Livingston	14,371	13,546	825	38,884	36,574	2,310
Logan	170	0	170	476	0	476
Lyon	7,462	5,175	2,287	20,377	13,973	6,404
Marshall	7,060	2,442	4,618	19,523	6,593	12,930
McCracken	334	0	334	935	0	935
McCreary	2,362	0	2,362	6,614	0	6,614
McLean	1,054	0	1,054	2,951	0	2,951
Metcalfe	541	0	541	1,515	0	1,515
Muhlenberg	4,594	2,896	1,698	12,573	7,819	4,754
Ohio	45,482	321	45,161	127,318	867	126,451
Trigg	11,318	6,696	4,622	31,021	18,079	12,942
Union	463	0	463	1,296	0	1,296
Whitley	5,867	587	5,280	16,369	1,585	14,784
Wolfe	25	25	0	68	68	0
All counties	323,891	57,201	266,690	901,178	154,447	746,731

[a] Counties with no pulpwood production are omitted.

Table A.12—Roundwood pulpwood production in Louisiana, 2007

Parish[a]	All species	Softwood	Hardwood	All species	Softwood	Hardwood
	standard cords			*green tons*		
Acadia	2,410	2,273	137	6,521	6,137	384
Allen	174,420	151,670	22,750	473,209	409,509	63,700
Ascension	7,680	1,151	6,529	21,389	3,108	18,281
Assumption	219	0	219	613	0	613
Avoyelles	23,960	5,545	18,415	66,534	14,972	51,562
Beauregard	297,925	273,260	24,665	806,864	737,802	69,062
Bienville	217,565	174,690	42,875	591,713	471,663	120,050
Bossier	110,614	49,967	60,647	304,723	134,911	169,812
Caddo	72,373	38,516	33,857	198,793	103,993	94,800
Calcasieu	75,543	75,531	12	203,968	203,934	34
Caldwell	88,177	78,235	9,942	239,073	211,235	27,838
Catahoula	31,327	23,515	7,812	85,365	63,491	21,874
Claiborne	78,697	59,361	19,336	214,416	160,275	54,141
Concordia	22,959	320	22,639	64,253	864	63,389
De Soto	239,741	199,884	39,857	651,287	539,687	111,600
East Baton Rouge	27,699	7,771	19,928	76,780	20,982	55,798
East Carroll	10,963	596	10,367	30,637	1,609	29,028
East Feliciana	66,837	44,539	22,298	182,689	120,255	62,434
Evangeline	25,678	25,011	667	69,398	67,530	1,868
Franklin	10,846	4,466	6,380	29,922	12,058	17,864
Grant	82,359	71,811	10,548	223,424	193,890	29,534
Iberia	530	30	500	1,481	81	1,400
Iberville	12,807	25	12,782	35,858	68	35,790
Jackson	224,758	178,107	46,651	611,512	480,889	130,623
Jefferson Davis	4,992	4,882	110	13,489	13,181	308
Lafayette	53	43	10	144	116	28
Lafourche	114	0	114	319	0	319
La Salle	169,650	138,925	30,725	461,128	375,098	86,030
Lincoln	53,512	36,754	16,758	146,158	99,236	46,922
Livingston	96,509	73,631	22,878	262,862	198,804	64,058
Madison	9,698	280	9,418	27,126	756	26,370
Morehouse	98,760	64,254	34,506	270,103	173,486	96,617
Natchitoches	241,751	200,658	41,093	656,837	541,777	115,060
Orleans	30	20	10	82	54	28
Ouachita	79,392	46,433	32,959	217,654	125,369	92,285
Plaquemines	11	11	0	30	30	0
Pointe Coupee	33,313	17	33,296	93,275	46	93,229
Rapides	152,651	126,626	26,025	414,760	341,890	72,870
Red River	67,029	54,594	12,435	182,222	147,404	34,818
Richland	7,221	456	6,765	20,173	1,231	18,942
Sabine	377,249	336,266	40,983	1,022,670	907,918	114,752
St. Bernard	22	22	0	59	59	0
St. Charles	945	0	945	2,646	0	2,646
St. Helena	69,894	53,745	16,149	190,329	145,112	45,217
St. James	4,668	0	4,668	13,070	0	13,070
St. John the Baptist	19,043	2,565	16,478	53,064	6,926	46,138

continued

Table A.12—Roundwood pulpwood production in Louisiana, 2007 (continued)

Parish[a]	All species	Softwood	Hardwood	All species	Softwood	Hardwood
	standard cords			*green tons*		
St. Martin	2,924	0	2,924	8,187	0	8,187
St. Tammany	84,800	83,234	1,566	229,117	224,732	4,385
Tangipahoa	79,381	53,715	25,666	216,896	145,031	71,865
Tensas	13,206	12	13,194	36,975	32	36,943
Union	147,783	90,391	57,392	404,754	244,056	160,698
Vermilion	123	123	0	332	332	0
Vernon	433,441	397,496	35,945	1,173,885	1,073,239	100,646
Washington	144,136	139,151	4,985	389,666	375,708	13,958
Webster	103,512	58,168	45,344	284,017	157,054	126,963
West Baton Rouge	7,953	156	7,797	22,253	421	21,832
West Carroll	6,625	4,164	2,461	18,134	11,243	6,891
West Feliciana	37,199	16,666	20,533	102,490	44,998	57,492
Winn	339,790	287,135	52,655	922,699	775,265	147,434
All parishes	4,793,467	3,736,867	1,056,600	13,048,027	10,089,547	2,958,480

[a] Parishes with no pulpwood production are omitted.

Table A.13—Roundwood pulpwood production in Mississippi, 2007

County[a]	All species	Softwood	Hardwood	All species	Softwood	Hardwood
	standard cords			*green tons*		
Adams	24,822	8,422	16,400	68,659	22,739	45,920
Alcorn	31,678	20,006	11,672	86,698	54,016	32,682
Amite	165,337	114,933	50,404	451,450	310,319	141,131
Attala	67,657	48,633	19,024	184,576	131,309	53,267
Benton	30,688	19,312	11,376	83,995	52,142	31,853
Bolivar	19,183	71	19,112	53,706	192	53,514
Calhoun	56,081	49,188	6,893	152,108	132,808	19,300
Carroll	64,988	41,984	23,004	177,768	113,357	64,411
Chickasaw	46,635	23,553	23,082	128,223	63,593	64,630
Choctaw	91,154	80,442	10,712	247,187	217,193	29,994
Claiborne	45,606	20,464	25,142	125,651	55,253	70,398
Clarke	130,953	93,816	37,137	357,287	253,303	103,984
Clay	21,637	19,163	2,474	58,667	51,740	6,927
Coahoma	2,368	9	2,359	6,629	24	6,605
Copiah	131,771	86,311	45,460	360,328	233,040	127,288
Covington	63,689	57,103	6,586	172,619	154,178	18,441
De Soto	6,806	6,779	27	18,379	18,303	76
Forrest	42,491	42,033	458	114,771	113,489	1,282
Franklin	54,483	34,664	19,819	149,086	93,593	55,493
George	38,622	38,622	0	104,279	104,279	0
Greene	146,053	127,765	18,288	396,172	344,966	51,206
Grenada	20,291	14,968	5,323	55,318	40,414	14,904
Hancock	42,434	42,222	212	114,593	113,999	594
Harrison	59,124	59,061	63	159,641	159,465	176
Hinds	104,973	51,044	53,929	288,820	137,819	151,001
Holmes	75,598	37,627	37,971	207,912	101,593	106,319
Humphreys	2,680	0	2,680	7,504	0	7,504
Issaquena	20,897	44	20,853	58,507	119	58,388
Itawamba	44,005	28,946	15,059	120,319	78,154	42,165
Jackson	43,438	43,429	9	117,283	117,258	25
Jasper	51,083	41,136	9,947	138,919	111,067	27,852
Jefferson	63,450	44,482	18,968	173,211	120,101	53,110
Jefferson Davis	49,850	49,842	8	134,595	134,573	22
Jones	75,424	56,668	18,756	205,521	153,004	52,517
Kemper	100,404	83,003	17,401	272,831	224,108	48,723
Lafayette	18,050	15,244	2,806	49,016	41,159	7,857
Lamar	53,738	46,087	7,651	145,858	124,435	21,423
Lauderdale	282,469	110,709	171,760	779,842	298,914	480,928
Lawrence	79,880	71,113	8,767	216,553	192,005	24,548
Leake	58,978	48,833	10,145	160,255	131,849	28,406
Lee	9,800	5,039	4,761	26,936	13,605	13,331
Leflore	1,907	11	1,896	5,339	30	5,309
Lincoln	314,830	198,765	116,065	861,648	536,666	324,982
Lowndes	125,104	20,437	104,667	348,248	55,180	293,068
Madison	72,485	50,420	22,065	197,916	136,134	61,782
Marion	116,667	64,571	52,096	320,211	174,342	145,869

continued

Table A.13—Roundwood pulpwood production in Mississippi, 2007 (continued)

County[a]	All species	Softwood	Hardwood	All species	Softwood	Hardwood
	standard cords			green tons		
Marshall	14,115	10,118	3,997	38,511	27,319	11,192
Monroe	90,576	30,860	59,716	250,527	83,322	167,205
Montgomery	44,477	19,709	24,768	122,564	53,214	69,350
Neshoba	66,176	43,077	23,099	180,985	116,308	64,677
Newton	53,766	32,579	21,187	147,287	87,963	59,324
Noxubee	83,135	82,123	1,012	224,566	221,732	2,834
Oktibbeha	38,970	37,783	1,187	105,338	102,014	3,324
Panola	60,409	24,612	35,797	166,684	66,452	100,232
Pearl River	144,768	124,905	19,863	392,860	337,244	55,616
Perry	114,980	111,921	3,059	310,752	302,187	8,565
Pike	44,244	34,722	9,522	120,411	93,749	26,662
Pontotoc	28,940	19,499	9,441	79,082	52,647	26,435
Prentiss	55,499	39,840	15,659	151,413	107,568	43,845
Quitman	21	21	0	57	57	0
Rankin	164,646	122,747	41,899	448,734	331,417	117,317
Scott	79,652	63,141	16,511	216,712	170,481	46,231
Sharkey	3,417	180	3,237	9,550	486	9,064
Simpson	67,712	59,211	8,501	183,673	159,870	23,803
Smith	173,089	163,054	10,035	468,344	440,246	28,098
Stone	96,716	96,716	0	261,133	261,133	0
Sunflower	8	0	8	22	0	22
Tallahatchie	6,949	3,584	3,365	19,099	9,677	9,422
Tate	8,328	7,712	616	22,547	20,822	1,725
Tippah	56,883	43,813	13,070	154,891	118,295	36,596
Tishomingo	58,732	48,607	10,125	159,589	131,239	28,350
Tunica	819	0	819	2,293	0	2,293
Union	26,277	17,671	8,606	71,809	47,712	24,097
Walthall	47,112	38,122	8,990	128,101	102,929	25,172
Warren	36,859	2,313	34,546	102,974	6,245	96,729
Washington	13,776	351	13,425	38,538	948	37,590
Wayne	175,549	101,772	73,777	481,360	274,784	206,576
Webster	38,060	29,291	8,769	103,639	79,086	24,553
Wilkinson	122,235	79,091	43,144	334,349	213,546	120,803
Winston	175,845	109,300	66,545	481,436	295,110	186,326
Yalobusha	27,635	23,361	4,274	75,042	63,075	11,967
Yazoo	31,201	9,204	21,997	86,443	24,851	61,592
All counties	5,421,837	3,747,984	1,673,853	14,806,349	10,119,557	4,686,792

[a] Counties with no pulpwood production are omitted.

Table A.14—Roundwood pulpwood production in North Carolina, 2007

County[a]	All species	Softwood	Hardwood	All species	Softwood	Hardwood
	standard cords			*green tons*		
Alamance	9,002	565	8,437	25,150	1,526	23,624
Alexander	1,829	2	1,827	5,121	5	5,116
Alleghany	6,633	69	6,564	18,565	186	18,379
Anson	88,397	77,320	11,077	239,780	208,764	31,016
Ashe	8,103	1,067	7,036	22,582	2,881	19,701
Beaufort	161,213	101,598	59,615	441,237	274,315	166,922
Bertie	154,148	111,769	42,379	420,437	301,776	118,661
Bladen	80,986	65,037	15,949	220,257	175,600	44,657
Brunswick	107,534	92,651	14,883	291,830	250,158	41,672
Buncombe	9,801	4,445	5,356	26,999	12,002	14,997
Burke	29,612	11,112	18,500	81,802	30,002	51,800
Cabarrus	6,213	5,980	233	16,798	16,146	652
Caldwell	2,208	119	2,089	6,170	321	5,849
Camden	36,555	4,893	31,662	101,865	13,211	88,654
Carteret	36,688	28,691	7,997	99,858	77,466	22,392
Caswell	21,920	146	21,774	61,361	394	60,967
Catawba	1,301	586	715	3,584	1,582	2,002
Chatham	7,606	2,563	5,043	21,040	6,920	14,120
Cherokee	47,878	20,336	27,542	132,025	54,907	77,118
Chowan	21,760	11,656	10,104	59,762	31,471	28,291
Clay	13,439	6,297	7,142	37,000	17,002	19,998
Cleveland	19,334	13,234	6,100	52,812	35,732	17,080
Columbus	100,122	75,042	25,080	272,837	202,613	70,224
Craven	115,566	76,629	38,937	315,922	206,898	109,024
Cumberland	33,473	18,267	15,206	91,898	49,321	42,577
Currituck	8,339	2,676	5,663	23,081	7,225	15,856
Dare	221	46	175	614	124	490
Davidson	2,497	379	2,118	6,953	1,023	5,930
Davie	1,906	29	1,877	5,334	78	5,256
Duplin	73,813	35,812	38,001	203,095	96,692	106,403
Durham	3,306	0	3,306	9,257	0	9,257
Edgecombe	63,706	37,862	25,844	174,590	102,227	72,363
Forsyth	3,408	641	2,767	9,479	1,731	7,748
Franklin	35,568	12,632	22,936	98,327	34,106	64,221
Gaston	9,588	3,173	6,415	26,529	8,567	17,962
Gates	100,392	60,117	40,275	275,086	162,316	112,770
Graham	7,856	0	7,856	21,997	0	21,997
Granville	29,742	74	29,668	83,270	200	83,070
Greene	14,693	5,256	9,437	40,615	14,191	26,424
Guilford	4,700	730	3,970	13,087	1,971	11,116
Halifax	109,302	58,476	50,826	300,198	157,885	142,313
Harnett	24,912	16,843	8,069	68,069	45,476	22,593
Haywood	37,220	12,223	24,997	102,994	33,002	69,992
Hertford	65,755	38,164	27,591	180,298	103,043	77,255
Hoke	24,739	19,892	4,847	67,280	53,708	13,572
Hyde	38,685	31,292	7,393	105,188	84,488	20,700
Iredell	9,162	325	8,837	25,622	878	24,744

continued

Table A.14—Roundwood pulpwood production in North Carolina, 2007 (continued)

County[a]	All species	Softwood	Hardwood	All species	Softwood	Hardwood
	standard cords			*green tons*		
Johnston	32,566	9,537	23,029	90,231	25,750	64,481
Jones	106,068	83,150	22,918	288,675	224,505	64,170
Lee	2,982	1,080	1,902	8,242	2,916	5,326
Lenoir	47,608	30,326	17,282	130,270	81,880	48,390
Lincoln	7,221	2,168	5,053	20,002	5,854	14,148
Macon	29,204	7,875	21,329	80,984	21,263	59,721
Martin	66,070	51,774	14,296	179,819	139,790	40,029
McDowell	29,217	13,505	15,712	80,458	36,464	43,994
Mecklenburg	13,206	2,540	10,666	36,723	6,858	29,865
Montgomery	82,688	19,131	63,557	229,614	51,654	177,960
Moore	39,536	28,818	10,718	107,819	77,809	30,010
Nash	29,597	10,666	18,931	81,805	28,798	53,007
New Hanover	3,380	2,723	657	9,192	7,352	1,840
Northampton	138,542	85,104	53,438	379,407	229,781	149,626
Onslow	127,871	104,321	23,550	347,607	281,667	65,940
Orange	1,357	0	1,357	3,800	0	3,800
Pamlico	70,445	44,464	25,981	192,800	120,053	72,747
Pasquotank	27,957	9,643	18,314	77,315	26,036	51,279
Pender	69,849	61,808	8,041	189,397	166,882	22,515
Perquimans	17,566	11,031	6,535	48,082	29,784	18,298
Person	27,403	33	27,370	76,725	89	76,636
Pitt	103,120	57,143	45,977	283,022	154,286	128,736
Polk	23,360	14,075	9,285	64,001	38,003	25,998
Randolph	5,259	1,715	3,544	14,554	4,631	9,923
Richmond	25,674	24,383	1,291	69,449	65,834	3,615
Robeson	77,812	44,265	33,547	213,448	119,516	93,932
Rockingham	61,990	11,081	50,909	172,464	29,919	142,545
Rowan	39,016	1,968	37,048	109,048	5,314	103,734
Rutherford	100,950	18,275	82,675	280,833	49,343	231,490
Sampson	52,745	33,995	18,750	144,287	91,787	52,500
Scotland	26,522	20,194	6,328	72,242	54,524	17,718
Stanly	12,894	12,047	847	34,899	32,527	2,372
Stokes	9,773	1,463	8,310	27,218	3,950	23,268
Surry	7,440	453	6,987	20,787	1,223	19,564
Tyrrell	30,446	15,381	15,065	83,711	41,529	42,182
Union	49,299	9,031	40,268	137,134	24,384	112,750
Vance	15,124	2,260	12,864	42,121	6,102	36,019
Wake	83,188	28,296	54,892	230,097	76,399	153,698
Warren	76,922	32,309	44,613	212,150	87,234	124,916
Washington	37,254	26,826	10,428	101,628	72,430	29,198
Watauga	1,505	56	1,449	4,208	151	4,057
Wayne	42,014	14,238	27,776	116,216	38,443	77,773
Wilkes	33,598	2,273	31,325	93,847	6,137	87,710
Wilson	26,323	13,113	13,210	72,393	35,405	36,988
Yadkin	3,750	209	3,541	10,479	564	9,915
All counties	3,707,142	2,031,462	1,675,680	10,176,858	5,484,950	4,691,908

[a] Counties with no pulpwood production are omitted.

Table A.15—Roundwood pulpwood production in Oklahoma, 2007

County[a]	All species	Softwood	Hardwood	All species	Softwood	Hardwood
	standard cords			*green tons*		
Adair	5,581	0	5,581	15,627	0	15,627
Atoka	1,633	791	842	4,494	2,136	2,358
Choctaw	14,642	6,866	7,776	40,311	18,538	21,773
Latimer	1,369	0	1,369	3,833	0	3,833
Le Flore	44,510	18,196	26,314	122,808	49,129	73,679
McCurtain	208,340	133,821	74,519	569,970	361,317	208,653
Pittsburg	2,035	2,035	0	5,495	5,495	0
Pushmataha	181,451	83,948	97,503	499,668	226,660	273,008
All counties	459,561	245,657	213,904	1,262,206	663,275	598,931

[a] Counties with no pulpwood production are omitted.

Table A.16—Roundwood pulpwood production in South Carolina, 2007

County[a]	All species	Softwood	Hardwood	All species	Softwood	Hardwood
	standard cords			green tons		
Abbeville	22,829	6,917	15,912	63,230	18,676	44,554
Aiken	93,270	67,793	25,477	254,377	183,041	71,336
Allendale	54,721	39,049	15,672	149,314	105,432	43,882
Anderson	17,510	1,443	16,067	48,884	3,896	44,988
Bamberg	62,230	43,516	18,714	169,892	117,493	52,399
Barnwell	42,082	34,820	7,262	114,348	94,014	20,334
Beaufort	35,823	28,125	7,698	97,492	75,938	21,554
Berkeley	194,106	173,690	20,416	526,128	468,963	57,165
Calhoun	31,594	23,081	8,513	86,155	62,319	23,836
Charleston	116,821	93,554	23,267	317,744	252,596	65,148
Cherokee	36,348	23,618	12,730	99,413	63,769	35,644
Chester	159,133	132,337	26,796	432,339	357,310	75,029
Chesterfield	118,110	87,432	30,678	321,964	236,066	85,898
Clarendon	48,814	37,544	11,270	132,925	101,369	31,556
Colleton	238,379	190,510	47,869	648,410	514,377	134,033
Darlington	36,007	18,949	17,058	98,924	51,162	47,762
Dillon	51,270	30,581	20,689	140,498	82,569	57,929
Dorchester	122,380	93,364	29,016	333,328	252,083	81,245
Edgefield	78,998	65,876	13,122	214,607	177,865	36,742
Fairfield	332,672	310,842	21,830	900,397	839,273	61,124
Florence	160,982	117,571	43,411	438,993	317,442	121,551
Georgetown	230,845	188,917	41,928	627,474	510,076	117,398
Greenville	33,014	18,773	14,241	90,562	50,687	39,875
Greenwood	24,249	19,260	4,989	65,971	52,002	13,969
Hampton	162,510	143,340	19,170	440,694	387,018	53,676
Horry	136,547	91,354	45,193	373,196	246,656	126,540
Jasper	98,746	65,016	33,730	269,987	175,543	94,444
Kershaw	147,662	124,667	22,995	400,987	336,601	64,386
Lancaster	138,111	119,637	18,474	374,747	323,020	51,727
Laurens	21,499	12,259	9,240	58,971	33,099	25,872
Lee	50,003	34,778	15,225	136,531	93,901	42,630
Lexington	40,875	31,992	8,883	111,250	86,378	24,872
Marion	74,780	37,070	37,710	205,677	100,089	105,588
Marlboro	80,677	59,951	20,726	219,901	161,868	58,033
McCormick	14,449	9,863	4,586	39,471	26,630	12,841
Newberry	104,201	100,646	3,555	281,698	271,744	9,954
Oconee	51,155	29,488	21,667	140,286	79,618	60,668
Orangeburg	196,285	150,437	45,848	534,554	406,180	128,374
Pickens	18,496	7,537	10,959	51,035	20,350	30,685
Richland	103,845	70,745	33,100	283,692	191,012	92,680
Saluda	66,215	62,547	3,668	179,147	168,877	10,270
Spartanburg	41,457	19,676	21,781	114,112	53,125	60,987
Sumter	117,356	71,115	46,241	321,486	192,011	129,475
Union	102,611	64,086	38,525	280,902	173,032	107,870
Williamsburg	156,446	104,427	52,019	427,606	281,953	145,653
York	78,468	53,921	24,547	214,319	145,587	68,732
All counties	4,344,581	3,312,114	1,032,467	11,833,618	8,942,710	2,890,908

[a] Counties with no pulpwood production are omitted.

Table A.17—Roundwood pulpwood production in Tennessee, 2007

County[a]	All species	Softwood	Hardwood	All species	Softwood	Hardwood
	standard cords			*green tons*		
Anderson	26,593	392	26,201	74,421	1,058	73,363
Bedford	10,611	9,595	1,016	28,752	25,907	2,845
Benton	22,757	17,524	5,233	61,967	47,315	14,652
Bledsoe	20,367	10,033	10,334	56,024	27,089	28,935
Blount	6,357	1,122	5,235	17,687	3,029	14,658
Bradley	19,834	14,336	5,498	54,101	38,707	15,394
Campbell	32,139	0	32,139	89,989	0	89,989
Cannon	3,092	133	2,959	8,644	359	8,285
Carroll	22,902	9,576	13,326	63,168	25,855	37,313
Chester	18,355	9,164	9,191	50,478	24,743	25,735
Claiborne	10,732	0	10,732	30,050	0	30,050
Cocke	1,313	698	615	3,607	1,885	1,722
Coffee	5,614	1,262	4,352	15,593	3,407	12,186
Crockett	160	113	47	437	305	132
Cumberland	39,046	14,025	25,021	107,927	37,868	70,059
Decatur	42,143	30,907	11,236	114,910	83,449	31,461
DeKalb	329	13	316	920	35	885
Dickson	15,203	0	15,203	42,568	0	42,568
Dyer	1,135	0	1,135	3,178	0	3,178
Fayette	6,865	2,339	4,526	18,988	6,315	12,673
Fentress	7,524	643	6,881	21,003	1,736	19,267
Franklin	21,401	271	21,130	59,896	732	59,164
Gibson	999	448	551	2,753	1,210	1,543
Giles	8,173	2,277	5,896	22,657	6,148	16,509
Grundy	65,212	16,969	48,243	180,896	45,816	135,080
Hamblen	27	8	19	75	22	53
Hamilton	18,984	15,897	3,087	51,566	42,922	8,644
Hardeman	34,748	13,410	21,338	95,953	36,207	59,746
Hardin	87,917	58,981	28,936	240,270	159,249	81,021
Hawkins	10,229	0	10,229	28,641	0	28,641
Haywood	185	68	117	512	184	328
Henderson	19,359	4,705	14,654	53,735	12,704	41,031
Henry	11,917	6,096	5,821	32,758	16,459	16,299
Hickman	78,591	6,137	72,454	219,441	16,570	202,871
Houston	14,812	87	14,725	41,465	235	41,230
Humphreys	33,926	13,557	20,369	93,637	36,604	57,033
Johnson	2,336	5	2,331	6,541	14	6,527
Knox	6,575	5,845	730	17,826	15,782	2,044
Lauderdale	30	0	30	84	0	84
Lawrence	41,557	26,590	14,967	113,701	71,793	41,908
Lewis	79,976	3,661	76,315	223,567	9,885	213,682
Lincoln	3,858	0	3,858	10,802	0	10,802
Loudon	4,993	4,649	344	13,515	12,552	963
Madison	11,702	2,725	8,977	32,494	7,358	25,136
Marion	62,061	30,298	31,763	170,741	81,805	88,936
Marshall	774	42	732	2,163	113	2,050

continued

Table A.17—Roundwood pulpwood production in Tennessee, 2007 (continued)

County[a]	All species	Softwood	Hardwood	All species	Softwood	Hardwood
	standard cords			*green tons*		
Maury	12,818	1,463	11,355	35,744	3,950	31,794
McMinn	45,043	31,557	13,486	122,965	85,204	37,761
McNairy	62,613	29,924	32,689	172,324	80,795	91,529
Meigs	16,349	10,027	6,322	44,775	27,073	17,702
Monroe	18,552	5,652	12,900	51,380	15,260	36,120
Montgomery	3,205	2,618	587	8,713	7,069	1,644
Moore	2,034	0	2,034	5,695	0	5,695
Morgan	6,280	17	6,263	17,582	46	17,536
Obion	6,444	77	6,367	18,036	208	17,828
Overton	3,788	146	3,642	10,592	394	10,198
Perry	81,468	5,143	76,325	227,596	13,886	213,710
Polk	16,759	8,094	8,665	46,116	21,854	24,262
Putnam	518	100	418	1,440	270	1,170
Rhea	27,634	16,378	11,256	75,738	44,221	31,517
Roane	2,592	142	2,450	7,243	383	6,860
Rutherford	19	0	19	53	0	53
Scott	28,877	0	28,877	80,856	0	80,856
Sequatchie	23,797	9,853	13,944	65,646	26,603	39,043
Sevier	687	166	521	1,907	448	1,459
Shelby	436	333	103	1,187	899	288
Smith	9	0	9	25	0	25
Stewart	29,631	13,297	16,334	81,637	35,902	45,735
Tipton	21	0	21	59	0	59
Union	3,774	1,110	2,664	10,456	2,997	7,459
Van Buren	21,712	12,271	9,441	59,567	33,132	26,435
Warren	8,030	110	7,920	22,473	297	22,176
Wayne	163,313	93,615	69,698	447,915	252,761	195,154
Weakley	20,717	11,988	8,729	56,809	32,368	24,441
White	21,412	8,938	12,474	59,060	24,133	34,927
All counties	1,561,945	597,620	964,325	4,313,690	1,613,579	2,700,111

[a] Counties with no pulpwood production are omitted.

Table A.18—Roundwood pulpwood production in Texas, 2007

County[a]	All species	Softwood	Hardwood	All species	Softwood	Hardwood
		standard cords			green tons	
Anderson	8,081	7,892	189	21,837	21,308	529
Angelina	127,262	90,178	37,084	347,316	243,481	103,835
Bowie	74,243	29,727	44,516	204,908	80,263	124,645
Camp	9,150	2,837	6,313	25,336	7,660	17,676
Cass	319,064	105,655	213,409	882,814	285,269	597,545
Cherokee	55,317	35,786	19,531	151,309	96,622	54,687
Franklin	4,796	799	3,997	13,349	2,157	11,192
Gregg	6,955	2,156	4,799	19,258	5,821	13,437
Hardin	95,282	63,835	31,447	260,407	172,355	88,052
Harris	169	79	90	465	213	252
Harrison	69,561	28,956	40,605	191,875	78,181	113,694
Henderson	91	8	83	254	22	232
Houston	22,513	6,904	15,609	62,346	18,641	43,705
Jasper	181,234	153,240	27,994	492,131	413,748	78,383
Jefferson	59	59	0	159	159	0
Lamar	7,413	11	7,402	20,756	30	20,726
Liberty	73,968	42,219	31,749	202,888	113,991	88,897
Madison	39	12	27	108	32	76
Marion	69,100	25,424	43,676	190,938	68,645	122,293
Montgomery	21,041	5,337	15,704	58,381	14,410	43,971
Morris	13,270	3,638	9,632	36,793	9,823	26,970
Nacogdoches	103,269	81,936	21,333	280,959	221,227	59,732
Newton	172,288	156,175	16,113	466,789	421,673	45,116
Orange	28,467	11,398	17,069	78,568	30,775	47,793
Panola	132,574	68,584	63,990	364,349	185,177	179,172
Polk	29,626	22,119	7,507	80,741	59,721	21,020
Red River	143,647	28,972	114,675	399,314	78,224	321,090
Rusk	29,355	11,879	17,476	81,006	32,073	48,933
Sabine	55,978	39,337	16,641	152,805	106,210	46,595
San Augustine	99,173	80,994	18,179	269,585	218,684	50,901
San Jacinto	40,978	18,102	22,876	112,928	48,875	64,053
Shelby	80,075	68,142	11,933	217,395	183,983	33,412
Smith	39,658	10,079	29,579	110,034	27,213	82,821
Titus	19,454	1,347	18,107	54,337	3,637	50,700
Trinity	1,515	1,515	0	4,091	4,091	0
Tyler	142,322	93,162	49,160	389,185	251,537	137,648
Upshur	42,430	18,761	23,669	116,928	50,655	66,273
Walker	17,984	5,353	12,631	49,820	14,453	35,367
Wood	22,035	7,042	14,993	60,993	19,013	41,980
All counties	2,359,436	1,329,649	1,029,787	6,473,455	3,590,052	2,883,403

[a] Counties with no pulpwood production are omitted.

Table A.19—Roundwood pulpwood production in Virginia, 2007

County[a]	All species	Softwood	Hardwood	All species	Softwood	Hardwood
	standard cords			*green tons*		
Accomack	98	47	51	270	127	143
Albemarle	26,181	17,366	8,815	71,570	46,888	24,682
Alleghany	20,846	2,698	18,148	58,099	7,285	50,814
Amelia	15,058	93	14,965	42,153	251	41,902
Amherst	22,957	8,489	14,468	63,430	22,920	40,510
Appomattox	28,128	18,083	10,045	76,950	48,824	28,126
Augusta	4,714	1,033	3,681	13,096	2,789	10,307
Bath	15,242	2,619	12,623	42,415	7,071	35,344
Bedford	29,919	4,703	25,216	83,303	12,698	70,605
Bland	3,072	83	2,989	8,593	224	8,369
Botetourt	28,670	6,199	22,471	79,656	16,737	62,919
Brunswick	125,710	97,637	28,073	342,224	263,620	78,604
Buchanan	53	0	53	148	0	148
Buckingham	171,062	112,292	58,770	467,744	303,188	164,556
Campbell	56,864	18,326	38,538	157,386	49,480	107,906
Caroline	30,520	24,798	5,722	82,977	66,955	16,022
Carroll	3,743	0	3,743	10,480	0	10,480
Charles City	8,830	7,581	1,249	23,966	20,469	3,497
Charlotte	67,933	31,325	36,608	187,080	84,578	102,502
Chesapeake	5,879	1,364	4,515	16,325	3,683	12,642
Chesterfield	15,010	11,680	3,330	40,860	31,536	9,324
Craig	11,911	1,516	10,395	33,199	4,093	29,106
Culpeper	7,485	5,008	2,477	20,458	13,522	6,936
Cumberland	52,570	31,172	21,398	144,078	84,164	59,914
Dickenson	80,754	7	80,747	226,111	19	226,092
Dinwiddie	91,891	73,408	18,483	249,954	198,202	51,752
Essex	1,789	1,614	175	4,848	4,358	490
Fairfax	7,996	1,401	6,595	22,249	3,783	18,466
Fauquier	3,693	2,447	1,246	10,096	6,607	3,489
Floyd	183	0	183	512	0	512
Fluvanna	22,447	15,415	7,032	61,311	41,621	19,690
Franklin	32,946	8,575	24,371	91,392	23,153	68,239
Frederick	10,025	5,027	4,998	27,567	13,573	13,994
Gloucester	118	98	20	321	265	56
Goochland	16,078	11,416	4,662	43,877	30,823	13,054
Grayson	1,068	0	1,068	2,990	0	2,990
Greene	516	9	507	1,444	24	1,420
Greensville	71,161	43,347	27,814	194,916	117,037	77,879
Halifax	40,630	1,693	38,937	113,595	4,571	109,024
Hampton	102	8	94	285	22	263
Hanover	30,886	27,557	3,329	83,725	74,404	9,321
Henrico	760	669	91	2,061	1,806	255
Henry	18,184	4,910	13,274	50,424	13,257	37,167
Highland	9,070	1,651	7,419	25,231	4,458	20,773
Isle of Wight	44,455	22,364	22,091	122,238	60,383	61,855
James City	525	95	430	1,461	257	1,204
King and Queen	7,644	6,066	1,578	20,796	16,378	4,418
King George	3,723	2,891	832	10,136	7,806	2,330
King William	15,860	15,525	335	42,856	41,918	938

continued

Table A.19—Roundwood pulpwood production in Virginia, 2007 (continued)

County[a]	All species	Softwood	Hardwood	All species	Softwood	Hardwood
	standard cords			*green tons*		
Lancaster	122	112	10	330	302	28
Lee	1,224	1,224	0	3,305	3,305	0
Loudoun	644	0	644	1,803	0	1,803
Louisa	18,784	12,417	6,367	51,354	33,526	17,828
Lunenburg	31,042	12,552	18,490	85,662	33,890	51,772
Madison	1,701	452	1,249	4,717	1,220	3,497
Mathews	38	38	0	103	103	0
Mecklenburg	27,171	8,017	19,154	75,277	21,646	53,631
Middlesex	36	36	0	97	97	0
Montgomery	2,794	80	2,714	7,815	216	7,599
Nelson	19,667	12,118	7,549	53,856	32,719	21,137
New Kent	470	284	186	1,288	767	521
Newport News	253	106	147	698	286	412
Northampton	54	0	54	151	0	151
Northumberland	1,775	0	1,775	4,970	0	4,970
Nottoway	33,795	19,202	14,593	92,705	51,845	40,860
Orange	12,209	7,649	4,560	33,420	20,652	12,768
Page	4,860	2,250	2,610	13,383	6,075	7,308
Patrick	43,075	7,487	35,588	119,861	20,215	99,646
Pittsylvania	106,915	37,688	69,227	295,594	101,758	193,836
Powhatan	39,606	29,694	9,912	107,928	80,174	27,754
Prince Edward	31,514	8,631	22,883	87,376	23,304	64,072
Prince George	19,577	16,153	3,424	53,200	43,613	9,587
Prince William	4,027	2,240	1,787	11,052	6,048	5,004
Pulaski	73	0	73	204	0	204
Rappahannock	169	0	169	473	0	473
Richmond	8,455	1,595	6,860	23,515	4,307	19,208
Roanoke	6,097	550	5,547	17,017	1,485	15,532
Rockbridge	30,371	6,279	24,092	84,411	16,953	67,458
Rockingham	2,503	911	1,592	6,918	2,460	4,458
Russell	1,719	0	1,719	4,813	0	4,813
Shenandoah	4,981	2,376	2,605	13,709	6,415	7,294
Smyth	2,742	11	2,731	7,677	30	7,647
Southampton	136,021	77,458	58,563	373,113	209,137	163,976
Spotsylvania	24,999	19,638	5,361	68,034	53,023	15,011
Stafford	9,617	2,733	6,884	26,654	7,379	19,275
Suffolk	49,129	26,080	23,049	134,953	70,416	64,537
Surry	42,164	32,015	10,149	114,858	86,441	28,417
Sussex	123,629	104,668	18,961	335,695	282,604	53,091
Tazewell	3,516	21	3,495	9,843	57	9,786
Virginia Beach	6,504	5,357	1,147	17,676	14,464	3,212
Warren	5,174	1,617	3,557	14,326	4,366	9,960
Washington	445	0	445	1,246	0	1,246
Westmoreland	3,130	3,130	0	8,451	8,451	0
Wise	534	0	534	1,495	0	1,495
Wythe	543	0	543	1,520	0	1,520
All counties	2,128,827	1,113,174	1,015,653	5,849,402	3,005,576	2,843,826

[a] Counties with no pulpwood production are omitted.

Table A.20—Softwood roundwood pulpwood movement between States, 2007

Southeast

Imported from	Exported to											Roundwood production
	FL	GA	NC	SC	VA	AL	MD	MS	PA	TN	Other[a]	
	standard cords											
Florida	2,512,630	487,426	0	0	0	92,393	0	946	0	0	0	3,093,395
Georgia	584,109	5,511,842	1,963	33,463	0	462,266	0	0	0	279,980	36,912	6,910,535
North Carolina	0	0	1,590,849	335,015	89,336	0	0	0	0	16,262	0	2,031,462
South Carolina	0	399,208	298,665	2,601,416	0	0	0	0	0	6,926	5,899	3,312,114
Virginia	0	0	173,569	273	777,285	0	102,121	0	53,612	0	6,314	1,113,174
Alabama	235,133	479,854	0	0	10	0	0	0	0	0	0	NA
Mississippi	2,281	0	0	0	0	0	0	0	0	0	0	NA
Tennessee	0	0	5	0	0	0	0	0	0	0	0	NA
West Virginia	0	0	0	0	2,799	0	0	0	0	0	0	NA
Roundwood receipts	3,334,153	6,878,330	2,065,051	2,970,167	869,430							16,460,680

Total Southeast receipts = 16,117,131

South Central

Imported from	Exported to												Roundwood production
	AL	AR	KY	LA	MS	OK	TN	TX	FL	GA	NC	Other[b]	
	standard cords												
Alabama	3,974,695	0	0	46	371,243	0	166,357	0	235,133	479,854	0	10	5,227,338
Arkansas	0	1,218,742	0	291,976	0	200,865	0	133,882	0	0	0	0	1,845,465
Kentucky	0	0	17,468	0	0	0	14,110	0	0	0	0	25,623	57,201
Louisiana	0	74,371	0	3,406,405	28,120	1,605	0	226,366	0	0	0	0	3,736,867
Mississippi	121,769	39,419	0	622,120	2,580,193	0	382,202	0	2,281	0	0	0	3,747,984
Oklahoma	0	21,810	0	0	0	223,745	0	102	0	0	0	0	245,657
Tennessee	78,181	0	13,495	0	0	0	496,344	0	0	0	5	9,595	597,620
Texas	0	97,789	0	216,503	0	106,138	0	909,219	0	0	0	0	1,329,649
Florida	92,393	0	0	0	9	4	6	0	0	0	0	0	NA
Georgia	462,266	0	0	0	0	30,151	279,980	0	0	0	0	0	NA
Illinois	0	0	2,535	0	0	0	0	0	0	0	0	0	NA
North Carolina	0	0	0	0	0	0	16,262	0	0	0	0	0	NA
South Carolina	0	0	0	0	0	0	6,926	0	0	0	0	0	NA
Other[c]	0	2	30	0	0	0	0	0	0	0	0	0	NA
Roundwood receipts	4,729,304	1,452,154	33,498	4,537,050	2,980,502	562,504	1,362,181	1,269,569					16,787,781

Total South Central receipts = 16,926,762

Note: Boxed numbers are retained roundwood volume processed by mills in the State in which it is harvested.

NA = not applicable.

[a] Other destinations include Ohio and Oklahoma.

[b] Other destinations include Ohio and Virginia.

[c] Other sources include Missouri.

Table A 21—Hardwood roundwood pulpwood movement between States, 2007

Southeast

Imported from	Exported to										Round-wood production
	FL	GA	NC	SC	VA	AL	MD	PA	TN	Other^a	
	standard cords										
Florida	135,710	58,245	0	0	0	13,448	0	0	0	0	207,403
Georgia	0	1,043,441	4,253	8,698	4,985	170,117	0	0	85,181	2,807	1,319,482
North Carolina	0	484	982,579	224,772	379,978	0	0	0	86,754	1,113	1,675,680
South Carolina	0	119,213	55,671	857,573	0	0	0	0	10	0	1,032,467
Virginia	0	1,483	17,549	282	861,353	0	47,289	7,546	79,617	534	1,015,653
Alabama	157	50,026	1,894	0	0	0	0	0	0	0	NA
Pennsylvania	0	0	0	0	5	(0)	01	0	0	0	NA
Tennessee	0	0	103,033	3,967	2,701	0	0	0	0	0	NA
West Virginia	0	0	0	0	155,870	0	0	0	0	0	NA
Other^b	0	0	0	0	5	50	02	0	0	0	NA
Roundwood receipts	135,867	1,272,892	1,164,979	1,095,292	1,405,940						5,250,685

Total Southeast receipts = 5,074,970

South Central

Imported from	Exported to													Round-wood production
	AL	AR	KY	LA	MS	OK	TN	TX	FL	GA	NC	SC	Other^c	
	standard cords													
Alabama	2,561,851	43	20,546	624	17	0	16,890	10	157	50,026	1,894	0	0	2,652,058
Arkansas	0	990,252	6,639	41,471	0	54,180	0	130,158	0	0	0	0	0	1,222,700
Kentucky	0	0	222,071	0	0	0	37,553	0	0	0	0	0	7,066	266,690
Louisiana	0	105,512	0	750,083	3,420	766	0	196,819	0	0	0	0	0	1,056,600
Mississippi	419,965	305,836	129,875	493,502	234,777	0	77,597	12,301	0	0	0	0	0	1,673,853
Oklahoma	0	99,011	0	0	0	104,442	0	10,451	0	0	0	0	0	213,904
Tennessee	353,301	27	191,079	0	0	0	310,217	0	0	0	103,033	3,967	2,701	964,325
Texas	0	250,339	0	53,798	0	61,029	0	664,621	0	0	0	0	0	1,029,787
Florida	13,448	0	0	0	0	0	0	0	0	0	0	0	0	NA
Georgia	170,117	0	0	0	0	2,807	85,181	0	0	0	0	0	0	NA
Illinois	0	0	12,775	0	0	0	0	0	0	0	0	0	0	NA
North Carolina	0	0	600	0	0	513	86,754	0	0	0	0	0	0	NA
South Carolina	0	0	0	0	0	0	1	00	0	0	0	0	0	NA
Other^d	0	19	57,410	0	0	0	79,617	0	0	0	0	0	0	NA
Roundwood receipts	3,518,682	1,751,039	640,995	1,339,478	238,214	223,737	693,819	1,014,360						9,079,917

Total South Central receipts = 9,420,324

Note: Boxed numbers are retained roundwood volume processed by mills in the State in which it is harvested.

NA = not applicable.

^a Other destinations include Kentucky and Oklahoma.

^b Other sources include Kentucky.

^c Other destinations include Ohio and Virginia.

^d Other sources include Indiana, Missouri, and Virginia.

Table A.22—Southern pulpmills, by process and capacity, 2007

Location	Map code[a]	Company	Pulping capacity, 24 hours				
			All processes	Sulfate	Groundwood and other mechanical	Semi-chemical	Soda and sulfite
					tons		
Alabama							
Clairborne[b]	[1,2,3]	Alabama River Companies	3,600	3,000	600	0	0
Jackson	[4]	Boise Cascade LLC	800	800	0	0	0
Courtland	[5]	International Paper Company	2,360	2,360	0	0	0
Demopolis	[6]	Rock-Tenn Company	1,100	1,100	0	0	0
Selma	[7]	International Paper Company	1,260	1,260	0	0	0
Naheola	[8]	Georgia-Pacific Corporation	1,100	1,100	0	0	0
Brewton	[9]	Georgia-Pacific Corporation	1,300	1,300	0	0	0
Coosa Pines	[10]	AbitibiBowater, Inc.	800	0	0	800	0
Pine Hill	[11]	Weyerhaeuser Company	2,000	1,350	0	650	0
Cottonton	[12]	MeadWestvaco Corporation	2,300	2,300	0	0	0
Stevenson	[13]	Smurfit-Stone Container Corporation	750	0	0	750	0
Prattville	[14]	International Paper Company	2,710	2,710	0	0	0
		Total	20,080	17,280	600	2,200	0
Arkansas							
Pine Bluff	[15]	Delta Natural Kraft	450	450	0	0	0
Ashdown	[16]	Domtar, Inc.	2,450	2,450	0	0	0
Crossett	[17]	Georgia-Pacific Corporation	1,600	1,600	0	0	0
Morrilton	[18]	Green Bay Packaging, Inc.	800	800	0	0	0
Pine Bluff	[19]	Evergreen Packaging, Inc.	1,550	1,370	180	0	0
McGehee	[20]	Potlatch Corporation	900	900	0	0	0
		Total	7,750	7,570	180	0	0
Florida							
Perry	[21]	Buckeye Florida, LP	1,200	1,200	0	0	0
Cantonment	[22]	International Paper Company	1,570	1,570	0	0	0
Palatka	[23]	Georgia-Pacific Corporation	1,500	1,500	0	0	0
Fernandina Beach	[24]	Rayonier, Inc.	475	0	0	0	475
Fernandina Beach	[25]	Smurfit-Stone Container Corporation	2,200	2,200	0	0	0
Panama City	[26]	Smurfit-Stone Container Corporation	1,635	1,635	0	0	0
		Total	8,580	8,105	0	0	475
Georgia							
Augusta	[27]	Augusta Newsprint Company	1,100	0	1,100	0	0
Augusta	[28]	International Paper Company	2,030	2,030	0	0	0
Brunswick	[29]	Georgia-Pacific Corporation	2,450	2,450	0	0	0
Cedar Springs	[30]	Georgia-Pacific Corporation	2,825	2,300	0	525	0
Rome	[31]	Temple-Inland, Inc.	2,250	2,250	0	0	0
Riceboro	[32]	Interstate Paper LLC	780	780	0	0	0
Jesup	[33]	Rayonier, Inc.	1,750	1,750	0	0	0
Valdosta	[34]	Packaging Corporation of America	1,420	1,420	0	0	0
Macon	[35]	Graphic Packaging International, Inc.	1,450	1,450	0	0	0
Savannah	[36]	International Paper Company	2,830	2,830	0	0	0
Oglethorpe	[37]	Weyerhaeuser Company	1,155	1,155	0	0	0
Port Wentworth	[38]	Weyerhaeuser Company	975	975	0	0	0
		Total	21,015	19,390	1,100	525	0

continued

Table A.22—Southern pulpmills, by process and capacity, 2007 (continued)

Location	Map code[a]	Company	Pulping capacity, 24 hours				
			All processes	Sulfate	Groundwood and other mechanical	Semi-chemical	Soda and sulfite
					tons		
Kentucky							
Wickliffe	[39]	NewPage Corporation	850	850	0	0	0
Hawesville	[40]	Domtar, Inc.	1,400	1,400	0	0	0
		Total	2,250	2,250	0	0	0
Louisiana							
DeRidder	[41]	Boise Cascade Corporation	1,975	1,300	675	0	0
Bogalusa	[42]	Temple-Inland, Inc.	2,150	2,150	0	0	0
Port Hudson	[43]	Georgia-Pacific Corporation	1,920	1,920	0	0	0
Bastrop	[44]	International Paper Company	1,220	1,220	0	0	0
Pineville	[45]	International Paper Company	1,100	1,100	0	0	0
Mansfield	[46]	International Paper Company	2,740	2,140	0	600	0
St. Francisville	[47]	Tembec, Inc.	705	705	0	0	0
West Monroe	[48]	Graphic Packaging International, Inc.	1,980	1,730	0	250	0
Hodge	[49]	Smurfit-Stone Container Corporation	1,500	1,500	0	0	0
Campti	[50]	Weyerhaeuser Company	1,050	1,050	0	0	0
		Total	16,340	14,815	675	850	0
Mississippi							
Monticello	[51]	Georgia-Pacific Corporation	2,500	2,500	0	0	0
New Augusta	[52]	Koch Industries	1,550	1,550	0	0	0
Vicksburg	[53]	International Paper Company	1,490	1,490	0	0	0
Grenada	[54]	AbitibiBowater, Inc.	750	0	750	0	0
Columbus	[55a]	Weyerhaeuser Company	1,450	1,450	0	0	0
Columbus	[55b]	Domtar, Inc.	350	0	350	0	0
		Total	8,090	6,990	1,100	0	0
North Carolina							
Roaring River	[56]	Louisiana-Pacific Corporation	475	0	475	0	0
Canton	[57]	Evergreen Packaging, Inc.	1,600	1,600	0	0	0
Roanoke Rapids	[58]	KapStone Paper and Packaging Corp.	1,630	1,630	0	0	0
Riegelwood	[59]	International Paper Company	1,730	1,730	0	0	0
New Bern	[60]	Weyerhaeuser Company	900	900	0	0	0
Plymouth	[61]	Domtar, Inc.	1,200	1,200	0	0	0
		Total	7,535	7,060	475	0	0
Oklahoma							
Pryor	[62]	Georgia-Pacific Gypsum LLC	50	0	50	0	0
Valliant	[63]	Weyerhaeuser Company	2,800	2,200	0	600	0
		Total	2,850	2,200	50	600	0
South Carolina							
Catawba	[64]	Abitibi Bowater, Inc.	2,100	1,500	600	0	0
Georgetown	[65]	International Paper Company	1,700	1,700	0	0	0
Hartsville	[66]	Sonoco Products Company	300	0	0	300	0
Florence	[67]	Smurfit-Stone Container Corporation	1,530	1,530	0	0	0
Eastover	[68]	International Paper Company	1,840	1,840	0	0	0
Charleston	[69]	MeadWestvaco Corporation	2,080	2,080	0	0	0
Bennettsville	[70]	Domtar, Inc.	1,000	1,000	0	0	0
		Total	10,550	9,650	600	300	0

continued   43

Table A.22—Southern pulpmills, by process and capacity, 2007 (continued)

Location	Map code[a]	Company	Pulping capacity, 24 hours				
			All processes	Sulfate	Groundwood and other mechanical	Semi-chemical	Soda and sulfite
			tons				
Tennessee							
Calhoun	[71]	AbitibiBowater, Inc.	1,450	1,000	450	0	0
New Johnsonville	[72]	Temple-Inland, Inc.	500	0	0	500	0
Kingsport	[73]	Domtar, Inc.	850	0	0	0	850
Counce	[74]	Packaging Corporation of America	1,950	1,950	0	0	0
Knoxville	[75]	Tamko Building Products, Inc.	125	0	125	0	0
		Total	4,875	2,950	575	500	850
Texas							
Texarkana	[76]	International Paper Company	1,630	1,630	0	0	0
Orange	[77]	Temple-Inland, Inc.	1,866	1,866	0	0	0
Diboll	[78]	Temple-Inland, Inc.	500	0	500	0	0
Silsbee	[79]	MeadWestvaco Corporation	1,850	1,850	0	0	0
		Total	5,846	5,346	500	0	0
Virginia							
Ashland	[80]	White Birch Paper Co.	880	0	880	0	0
West Point	[81]	Smurfit-Stone Container Corporation	1,700	1,700	0	0	0
Jarratt	[82]	Georgia-Pacific Corporation	400	0	400	0	0
Big Island	[83]	Georgia-Pacific Corporation	864	0	0	864	0
Hopewell	[84]	Smurfit-Stone Container Corporation	1,030	1,030	0	0	0
Franklin	[85]	International Paper Company	2,230	2,230	0	0	0
Riverville	[86]	Greif Packaging, LLC	600	0	0	600	0
Covington	[87]	MeadWestvaco Corporation	2,100	2,100	0	0	0
		Total	9,804	7,060	1,280	1,464	0
Total South			125,565	110,666	7,135	6,439	1,325

[a] Corresponds to numbers at locations on the mill capacity map (fig. 7).
[b] This is pulping capacity for three mills at this site.

Table A.23—Other mills using southern pulpwood in 2007, by process and capacity

Location	Company	Pulping capacity, 24 hours				
		All processes	Sulfate	Groundwood and other mechanical	Semi-chemical	Soda and sulfite
		tons				
Maryland						
Luke	NewPage Corporation	850	850			
Ohio						
Chillicothe	Glatfelter Company	1,785	1,785			
Pennsylvania						
Spring Grove	Glatfelter Company	700	700			

www.ingramcontent.com/pod-product-compliance
Lightning Source LLC
Chambersburg PA
CBHW081124280526

45787CB00007B/2971